A HAPPY POEM TO END
EVERY DAY

A HAPPY POEM TO END EVERY DAY

EDITED BY *Jane McMorland Hunter*

BATSFORD

For John,
and obviously for Matilda,
with all my love.

First published in the United Kingdom in 2022 by

B. T. Batsford Ltd
43 Great Ormond Street
London
WC1N 3HZ

An imprint of B. T. Batsford Holdings Limited

ISBN 978 1 84994 720 6

A CIP catalogue record for this book
is available from the British Library.

10 9 8 7 6 5 4 3 2 1

Reproduction by Rival Colour Ltd, UK
Printed and bound by Toppan Leefung Printing Ltd, China

Illustrations by Holly Astle

CONTENTS

Introduction

Lodged in the airy world of the imagination, happiness is almost impossible to pin down in a hard and fast definition. What brings happiness to one person can cause boredom or even dislike in another. Equally there are many levels of happiness: gentle contentment, wild joy, lasting pleasure or fleeting moments of delight.

While I was compiling this anthology an article appeared in a newspaper giving a complicated scientific formula for happiness. Learned neuroscientists had worked out that in order to be happy one should lower one's expectations, to avoid disappointment, but not lower them so much that one becomes miserable. It is clearly a delicate balance. The other discovery they made is that happiness doesn't last long; it seems our brains adjust to a happy situation very quickly so we are ready to make the next move in life. Perhaps the best policy is to follow Iris Murdoch's advice and aim for a life with 'continuous small treats'. A daily poem (with one or two pieces of prose) will, I hope, bring readers of this collection continuous small slivers of happiness.

Love is probably the most popular poetic (and other) route to happiness, but this in itself is often unreliable and even short-lived. Friends, particularly old friends, are often regarded as more reliable bringers of happiness, but for some people, such as the aged subject of Leigh Hunt's poem 'Rondeau', one kiss is all it takes.

Nature is a more dependable source of joy, with each season bringing its own pleasures: skating and sledging on a snowy day, idly boating along a quiet river in summer, walking through leaves or huddling beside a fire in winter. Gardens and gardening, travel, dancing and sport (as long as you win, usually) all bring pleasure to some, as do driving, eating, drinking (in moderation) and listening to music. For those who find joy in the kitchen there are rhyming recipes for a cake and a salad, as well as advice on making the perfect margarita. Also included is one poet who finds pleasure in an unwreckable, impeccable, watertight lie! As with many things in life, happiness depends on the individual.

Animals can bring us great pleasure, but what of their feelings? While this anthology is primarily concerned with human happiness, I have included gardening guinea pigs, contented cats and a wildly ecstatic dog, and as spring takes hold an old and ragged crow enjoys the morning sunshine from the top of an ash tree.

Childhood is usually felt to be a happy time; Christina Rossetti magically describes a little girl who dances, sings and laughs despite her poverty, and for Laurence Binyon's little dancers, nothing in the outside world matters. Old age, though, divides poets; for some it is surprisingly pleasant, with many fears unfounded and a heightened sense of delight in each day. Others feel that it is more important to enjoy the benefits of youth while you can, 'Youth's the season made for joy ... Let's be gay, While we may ... Ours is not to-morrow' (John Gay, *The Beggar's Opera*).

Just as memories can bring happiness, so too can anticipation. Night-time assignations for Robert Browning and Edward Thomas are filled with expectancy and the hope of an evening, or longer, with a loved one.

Hope, while not necessarily the same as happiness, is closely entwined with it; on a daily basis each evening can provide time for reflection and each morning the opportunity for a new start.

Funny poems are not always happy; the humour is often at someone's expense. However I have included one or two humorous poems, such as the description of the relative states of the felon and the hapless constable in W. S. Gilbert's song or the happiness of Prebendary Gorm, only gained by the unfortunate demise of Mrs Gorm, in Harry Graham's short and bittersweet rhyme.

In the past it was often felt that a virtuous life would bring happiness, but this was probably rarely true in reality. Thomas Campion paints an idyllic picture of rural life but I am not sure the working farmers and shepherds would have agreed with him. It may have helped that many poets lived at a stage removed from the hardships of agricultural life and at times viewed the countryside through rose-tinted spectacles. Wealth is divisive regardless of occupation, with many poets in favour of a simple life, while A. H. Clough is convinced that it improves life immeasurably with his repeated refrain 'How pleasant it is to have money'. Alexander Pope and Thomas May favour a quiet life, while D. H. Lawrence and Rachel Field go one step further, writing on the delights of being alone. Friends or a partner, both or neither – all variations have their poetic supporters. For some, though, it doesn't seem to matter; the delightful subject of Laurence Alma-Tadema's poem has a cunning contingency plan.

I think, perhaps, a lot depends upon how happy the poet is in themselves. Situations that W. H. Davies would regard with joy would be tinged with sadness in A. E. Housman's eyes. Equally, W. S. Calverley's journey from Dover to Munich might, in another poet's view, have been intolerably uncomfortable. G. K. Chesterton's drunken travellers who made 'the rolling English road' are clearly set to have a good time, regardless of how lost they get en route: 'For there is good news yet to hear and fine things to be seen'.

One thing poets and scientists seem agreed upon is that happiness is fleeting – the moment should be seized. Gentle or exhilarating, it doesn't matter, these moments make life better.

Between the dusk of a summer night
　And the dawn of a summer day,
We caught at a mood as it passed in flight
　And we bade it stoop and stay.

W. E. Henley, from 'Praeludium', XXII

JANUARY

Winter Songs of Birds and Poets

The New Year

I am the little New Year, ho, ho!

Here I come tripping it over the snow.
Shaking my bells with a merry din –
So open your doors and let me in!

Presents I bring for each and all –
Big folks, little folks, short and tall;
Each one from me a treasure may win –
So open your doors and let me in!

Some shall have silver and some shall have gold,
Some shall have new clothes and some shall have old;
Some shall have brass and some shall have tin –
So open your doors and let me in!

Some shall have water and some shall have milk,
Some shall have satin and some shall have silk!
But each from me a present may win –
So open your doors and let me in!

Anon

Song in the Wood

FROM *THE LITTLE FRENCH LAWYER*, ACT IV, SCENE VI

This way, this way, come and hear,
You that hold these pleasures dear,
Fill your ears with our sweet sound,
Whilst we melt the frozen ground:
This way come, make haste oh fair!
Let your clear eyes gild the air;
Come and bless us with your sight,
This way, this way, seek delight.

Francis Beaumont (1584–1616) and John Fletcher (1579–1625)

Velvet Shoes

Let us walk in the white snow
  In a soundless space;
With footsteps quiet and slow,
  At a tranquil pace,
  Under veils of white lace.

I shall go shod in silk,
  And you in wool,
White as white cow's milk,
  More beautiful
  Than the breast of a gull.

We shall walk through the still town
  In a windless peace;
We shall step upon white down,
  Upon silver fleece,
  Upon softer than these.

We shall walk in velvet shoes:
  Wherever we go
Silence will fall like dews
  On white silence below.
  We shall walk in the snow.

Elinor Wylie (1885–1928)

The Bright Field

I have seen the sun break through
to illuminate a small field
for a while, and gone my way
and forgotten it. But that was the pearl
of great price, the one field that had
the treasure in it. I realize now
that I must give all that I have
to possess it. Life is not hurrying

on to a receding future, nor hankering after
an imagined past. It is the turning
aside like Moses to the miracle
of the lit bush, to a brightness
that seemed as transitory as your youth
once, but is the eternity that awaits you.

R. S. Thomas (1913–2000)

Balloons

Journeying on high, the silken castle glides,
Bright as a meteor through the azure tides;
O'er towns and towers and temples wins its way,
Or mounts sublime, and gilds the vault of day.
Silent with upturn'd eyes unbreathing crowds
Pursue the floating wonder to the clouds;
And, flush'd with transport or benumb'd with fear,
Watch, as it rises, the diminish'd sphere.
– Now less and less! – and now a speck is seen! –
And now the fleeting rack obtrudes between! –
With bended knees, raised arms, and suppliant brow
To every shrine with mingled cries they vow.
– 'Save Him, ye Saints! who o'er the good preside;
'Bear Him, ye Winds! ye Stars benignant! guide.'
 – The calm Philosopher in ether fails,
Views broader stars, and breathes in purer gales;
Sees, like a map, in many a waving line
Round Earth's blue plains her lucid waters mine;
Sees at his feet the forky lightnings glow,
And hears innocuous thunders roar below.

Erasmus Darwin (1731–1802)

Winter

FROM *THE SEASONS*, VERSE 2

Winter is a social season;
  Then we gather round the fire;
Books and pictures then delight us
  Fun and feasting mirth inspire.

Sara Coleridge (1802–1852)

Ice on the Highway

Seven buxom women abreast, and arm in arm,
   Trudge down the hill, tip-toed,
     And breathing warm;
They must perforce trudge thus, to keep upright
   On the glassy ice-bound road,
And they must get to market whether or no,
   Provisions running low
    With the nearing Saturday night,
While the lumbering van wherein they mostly ride
   Can nowise go:
Yet loud their laughter as they stagger and slide!

Yell'ham Hill

Thomas Hardy (1840–1928)

Skating in the Evening

FROM *THE PRELUDE*, 1850, BOOK FIRST

And in the frosty season, when the sun
Was set, and visible for many a mile
The cottage windows blazed through the twilight gloom,
I heeded not their summons: happy time
It was indeed for all of us – for me
It was a time of rapture! Clear and loud
The village clock tolled six, – I wheeled about,
Proud and exalting like an untired horse
That cares not for his home. All shod with steel.
We hissed along the polished ice in games
Confederate, imitative of the chase
And woodland pleasures, – the resounding horn,
The pack loud chiming, and the hunted hare.
So through the darkness and the cold we flew,
And not a voice was idle; with the din
Smitten, the precipices rang aloud;
The leafless trees and every icy crag
Tinkled like iron; while far distant hills
Into the tumult sent an alien sound
Of melancholy not unnoticed, while the stars
Eastward were sparkling clear, and in the west

The orange sky of evening died away.
Not seldom from the uproar I retired
Into a silent bay, or sportively
Glanced sideway, leaving the tumultuous throng,
To cut across the reflex of a star
That fled, and, flying still before me, gleamed
Upon the glassy plain; and oftentimes,
When we had given our bodies to the wind,
And all the shadowy banks on either side
Came sweeping through the darkness, spinning still
The rapid line of motion, then at once
Have I, reclining back upon my heels,
Stopped short; yet still the solitary cliffs
Wheeled by me – even as if the earth had rolled
With visible motion her diurnal round!
Behind me they did stretch in solemn train,
Feebler and feebler, and I stood and watched
Till all was tranquil as in a dreamless sleep.

William Wordsworth (1770–1850)

January

For January I give you vests of skins.
  And mighty fires in hall, and torches lit;
  Chambers and happy beds with all things fit;
Smooth silken sheets, rough furry counterpanes;
And sweetmeats baked; and one that deftly spins
  Warm arras; and Douay cloth, and store of it;
  And on this merry manner still to twit
The wind, when most his mastery the wind wins.
Or issuing forth at seasons in the day,
  Ye'll fling soft handfuls of the fair white snow
Among the damsels standing round, in play:
  And when you all are tired and all aglow,
  And the free Fellowship continue so.

Folgóre da San Gimignano (c. 1270–c. 1332)
Translated by Dante Gabriel Rossetti (1828–1882)

How Long I Sail'd

How long I sail'd, and never took a thought
To what port I was bound! Secure as sleep,
I dwelt upon the bosom of the deep
And perilous sea. And though my ship was fraught
With rare and precious fancies, jewels brought
From fairy-land, no course I cared to keep,
Nor changeful wind nor tide I heeded ought,
But joy'd to feel the merry billows leap,
And watch the sunbeams dallying with the waves;
Or haply dream what realms beneath may lie
Where the clear ocean is an emerald sky,
And mermaids warble in their coral caves,
Yet vainly woo me to their secret home; –
And sweet it were for ever so to roam.

Hartley Coleridge (1796–1849)

Metaphor of Sunshine

Heaven runs over
With sunshine which is poured into the brain
Of birds and poets, and kept for winter song;
And into flints to strike fire.

Thomas Lovell Beddoes (1803–1849)

The Dancers

The dancers danced in a quiet meadow
It was winter, the soft light lit on clouds
Of growing morning – their feet on the firm
Hill-side sounded like a baker's business
Heard from the yard of his beamy barn-grange.
One piped, and the measured irregular riddle
Of the dance ran onward in tangling threads,
A thing of the village, centuries old in charm,
With tunes from the earth they trod, and naturalness
Sweet like the need of pleasure of change.
For a lit room with panels gleaming
They practised this set by winter's dreaming
Of pictures as lovely as are in Spring's range ...
No candles, but the keen dew drops shining,
And only the far jolly barking of the dogs strange.

Ivor Gurney (1890–1937)

Winter Heavens

Sharp is the night, but stars with frost alive
Leap off the rim of earth across the dome.
It is a night to make the heavens our home
More than the nest whereto apace we strive.
Lengths down our road each fir-tree seems a hive,
In swarms outrushing from the golden comb.
They waken waves of thoughts that burst to foam:
The living throb in me, the dead revive.
Yon mantle clothes us: there, past mortal breath,
Life glistens on the river of the death.
It folds us, flesh and dust; and have we knelt,
Or never knelt, or eyed as kine the springs
Of radiance, the radiance enrings:
And this is the soul's haven to have felt.

George Meredith (1828–1909)

Puss

Puss loves man's winter fire
Now that the sun so soon
Leaves the hours cold it warmed
In burning June.

She purrs full length before
The heaped-up hissing blaze,
Drowsy in slumber down
Her head she lays.

While he with whom she dwells
Sits snug in his inglenook,
Stretches his legs to the flame
And reads his book.

Walter de la Mare (1873–1956)

The Heart of a Man

FROM *THE BEGGAR'S OPERA*, ACT II, SCENE IV, AIR IV

If the Heart of a Man is depressed with cares,
The mist is dispelled when a woman appears,
Like the notes of a fiddle, she sweetly, sweetly,
Raises the spirits, and charms our ears,
Roses and lilies her cheeks disclose,
But her ripe lips are more sweet than those
Press her,
Caress her,
With blisses,
Her kisses
Dissolve us in pleasure, and soft repose.

John Gay (1685–1732)

Ode on Solitude

Happy the man whose wish and care
    A few paternal acres bound,
Content to breathe his native air,
      In his own ground.

Whose herds with milk, whose fields with bread,
    Whose flocks supply him with attire,
Whose trees in summer yield him shade,
      In winter fire.

Blest, who can unconcern'dly find
    Hours, days, and years slide soft away,
In health of body, peace of mind,
      Quiet by day,

Sound sleep by night; study and ease,
    Together mixt; sweet recreation;
And Innocence, which most does please
      With meditation.

Thus let me live, unseen, unknown,
    Thus unlamented let me die,
Steal from the world, and not a stone
      Tell where I lie.

Alexander Pope (1688–1744)

A Country Boy in Winter

VERSES 1–3

The wind may blow the snow about,
  For all I care, says Jack,
And I don't mind how cold it grows,
  For then the ice won't crack.
Old folks may shiver all day long,
  But I shall never freeze;
What cares a jolly boy like me
  For winter days like these?

Far down the long snow-covered hills
  It is such fun to coast,
So clear the road! the fastest sled
  There is in school I boast.
The paint is pretty well worn off,
  But then I take the lead;
A dandy sled's a loiterer,
  And I go in for speed.

When I go home at supper-time,
  Ki! but my cheeks are red!
They burn and sting like anything;
  I'm cross until I'm fed.
You ought to see the biscuit go,
  I am so hungry then;
And old Aunt Polly says that boys
  Eat twice as much as men.

Sarah Orne Jewett (1849–1909)

England

We have no grass locked up in ice so fast
That cattle cut their faces and at last,
When it is reached, must lie them down and starve,
With bleeding mouths that freeze too hard to move.
We have not that delirious state of cold
That makes men warm and sing when in Death's hold.
We have no roaring floods whose angry shocks
Can kill the fishes dashed against the rocks.
We have no winds that cut down street by street,
As easy as our scythes can cut down wheat.
No mountains here to spew their burning hearts
Into the valleys, on our human parts.
No earthquakes here, that ring church bells afar,
A hundred miles from where those earthquakes are.
We have no cause to set our dreaming eyes,
Like Arabs, on fresh streams in Paradise.
We have no wilds to harbour men that tell
More murders than they can remember well.
No woman here shall wake from her night's rest,
To find a snake is sucking at her breast.
Though I have travelled many and many a mile,
And had a man to clean my boots and smile
With teeth that had less bone in them than gold –
Give me this England now for all my world.

W. H. Davies (1871–1940)

After the Lunch

On Waterloo Bridge where we said our goodbyes,
The weather conditions bring tears to my eyes.
I wipe them away with a black woolly glove
And try not to notice I've fallen in love.

On Waterloo Bridge I am trying to think:
This is nothing, you're high on the charm and the drink.
But the juke-box inside me is playing a song
That says something different. And when was it wrong?

On Waterloo Bridge with the wind in my hair
I am tempted to skip. *You're a fool.* I don't care.
The head does its best but the heart is the boss –
I admit it before I am halfway across.

Wendy Cope (1945–)

The Owl and the Pussycat

The Owl and the Pussycat went to sea
    In a beautiful pea-green boat,
They took some honey, and plenty of money,
    Wrapped up in a five-pound note.
The Owl looked up to the stars above,
    And sang to a small guitar,
'O lovely Pussy! O Pussy, my love,
    What a beautiful Pussy you are,
        You are,
        You are!
    What a beautiful Pussy you are!'

Pussy said to the Owl, 'You elegant fowl!
    How charmingly sweet you sing!
O let us be married! too long we have tarried:
    But what shall we do for a ring?'
They sailed away, for a year and a day,
    To the land where the Bong-tree grows,
And there in a wood a Piggy-wig stood,
    With a ring at the end of his nose,
        His nose,
        His nose.
    With a ring at the end of his nose.

'Dear Pig, are you willing to sell for one shilling
   Your ring?' Said the Piggy, 'I will.'
So they took it away and were married next day
   By the Turkey who lives on the hill.
They dined on mince, and slices of quince,
   Which they ate with a runcible spoon;
And hand in hand, on the edge of the sand
   They danced by the light of the moon,
     The moon,
     The moon,
   They danced by the light of the moon.

Edward Lear (1812–1888)

The Optimist

The optimist builds himself safe inside a cell
and paints the inside walls sky-blue
and blocks up the door
and says he's in heaven.

D. H. Lawrence (1885–1930)

Getting Older

The first surprise: I like it.
Whatever happens now, some things
that used to terrify have not:

I didn't die young, for instance. Or lose
my only love. My three children
never had to run away from anyone.

Don't tell me this gratitude is complacent.
We all approach the edge of the same blackness
which for me is silent.

Knowing as much sharpens
my delight in January freesia,
hot coffee, winter sunlight. So we say

as we lie close on some gentle occasion:
every day won from such
darkness is a celebration.

Elaine Feinstein (1930–2019)

If No One Ever Marries Me

If no one ever marries me –
    And I don't see why they should,
For nurse says I'm not pretty
    And I'm seldom very good –

If no one ever marries me
    I shan't mind very much;
I shall buy a squirrel in a cage,
    And a little rabbit hutch.

I shall have a cottage near a wood,
    And a pony all my own,
And a little lamb, quite clean and tame,
    That I can take to town.

And when I'm getting really old,
    At twenty-eight or nine,
I shall buy a little orphan girl
    And bring her up as mine.

Laurence Alma-Tadema (c. 1865–1940)

A Task Done

FROM *A WINTER'S DAY: MORNING*

The cock, warm roosting midst his feathered dames,
Now lifts his beak and snuffs the morning air,
Stretches his neck and claps his heavy wings,
Gives three hoarse crows and, glad his task is done,
Low-chuckling turns himself upon the roost,
Then nestles down again amongst his mates.

Joanna Baillie (1762–1851)

A Grace Before Dinner

O Thou, who kindly dost provide
   For every creature's want!
We bless thee, God of Nature wide,
   For all thy goodness lent:
And, if it please thee, Heavenly Guide,
   May never worse be sent;
But whether granted, or denied,
   Lord, bless us with content!
                Amen!

Robert Burns (1759–1796)

On First Looking into Chapman's Homer

Much have I travell'd in the realms of gold,
  And many goodly states and kingdoms seen;
  Round many western islands have I been
Which bards in fealty to Apollo hold.
Oft of one wide expanse had I been told
  That deep-brow'd Homer ruled as his demesne;
  Yet did I never breathe its pure serene
Till I heard Chapman speak out loud and bold:
Then felt I like some watcher of the skies
  When a new planet swims into his ken;
Or like stout Cortez when with eagle eyes
  He star'd at the Pacific – and all his men
Look'd at each other with a wild surmise –
  Silent, upon a peak in Darien.

John Keats (1795–1821)

To Enjoy

FROM *THE TRAGEDY OF CLEOPATRA*

Not he that knows how to acquire,
    But to enjoy, is blest.
Nor does our happiness consist
    In motion, but in rest.

The gods pass man in bliss, because
They toil not for more height;
But can enjoy, and in their own
    Eternal rest delight.

Then, princes, do not toil nor care
    Enjoy what you possess.
Which whilst you do, you equalize
The gods in happiness.

Thomas May (1594/5–1650)

Travel

The railroad track is miles away,
  And the day is loud with voices speaking,
Yet there isn't a train goes by all day
  But I hear its whistle shrieking.

All night there isn't a train goes by,
  Though the night is still for sleep and dreaming,
But I see its cinders red on the sky,
  And hear its engine steaming.

My heart is warm with the friends I make,
  And better friends I'll not be knowing,
Yet there isn't a train I wouldn't take,
  No matter where it's going.

Edna St Vincent Millay (1892–1950)

All Shall be Well

FROM *REVELATIONS OF DIVINE LOVE*, THE THIRTEENTH REVELATION

'Often I wondered why by the great foreseeing wisdom
of God the beginning of sin was not hindered: for then,
methought, all should have been well.'

. . . .

And thus our good Lord answered to all the questions
and doubts that I might make, saying full comfortably:
I may make all thing well, I can make all thing well,
I will make all thing well, and I shall make all thing
well; and thou shalt see thyself that all manner of
thing shall be well.

Julian of Norwich (1342–c. 1430)
Edited by Grace Warwick (1855–1932)

Fire-side Enjoyments

FROM *THE TASK*, BOOK IV, LINES 120–143

Oh Winter! ruler of th' inverted year,
Thy scatter'd hair with sleet like ashes fill'd,
Thy breath congeal'd upon thy lips, thy cheeks
Fring'd with a beard made white with other snows
Than those of age; thy forehead wrapt in clouds,
A leafless branch thy sceptre, and thy throne
A sliding car, indebted to no wheels,
But urg'd by storms along its slipp'ry way;
I love thee, all unlovely as thou seem'st,
And dreaded as thou art! Thou hold'st the sun
A pris'ner in the yet undawning east,
Short'ning his journey between morn and noon,
And hurrying him, impatient of his stay,
Down to the rosy west; but kindly still
Compensating his loss with added hours
Of social converse and instructive ease,
And gath'ring at short notice, in one group,
The family dispers'd, and fixing thought,
Not less dispers'd by day-light and its cares.
I crown thee king of intimate delights,
Fire-side enjoyments, home-born happiness,
And all the comforts that the lowly roof
Of undisturb'd retirement, and the hours
Of long uninterrupted evening, know.

William Cowper (1731–1800)

L'amitié, est L'amour sans Ailes

VERSE 1

Why should my anxious breast repine,
Because my youth is fled?
Days of delight may still be mine;
Affection is not dead.
In tracing back the years of youth,
One firm record, one lasting truth
Celestial consolation brings;
Bear it, ye breezes, to the seat,
Where first my heart responsive beat, –
'Friendship is Love without his wings!'

George Gordon, Lord Byron (1788–1824)

FEBRUARY

Gather Round the Fire

At Night

Love said, 'Lie still and think of me,'
　Sleep, 'Close your eyes till break of day,'
But Dreams came by and smilingly
　Gave both to Love and Sleep their way.

Sara Teasdale (1884–1933)

Upon a Rare Voice

When I but hear her sing, I fare
Like one that, raised, holds his ear
To some bright star in the supremest round,
Through which, besides the light that's seen,
There may be heard from heaven within
The rests of anthems that the angels sound.

Owen Feltham (c. 1602–1668)

Flowers in Winter

PAINTED UPON A PORTE LIVRE, VERSES 1–3

How strange to greet, this frosty morn,
  In graceful counterfeit of flower,
These children of the meadows, born
  Of sunshine and of showers!

How well the conscious wood retains
  The pictures of its flower-sown home, –
The lights and shades, the purple stains,
  And golden hues of bloom!

It was a happy thought to bring
  To the dark season's frost and rime
This painted memory of spring,
  This dream of summer-time.

John Greenleaf Whittier (1807–1892)

To Jane: The Invitation

Best and brightest, come away!
Fairer far than this fair Day,
Which, like thee to those in sorrow,
Comes to bid a sweet good-morrow
To the rough Year just awake
In its cradle on the brake
The brightest hour of unborn Spring,
Through the winter wandering,
Found, it seems, the halcyon Morn
To hoar February born.
Bending from Heaven, in azure mirth,
It kiss'd the forehead of the Earth,
And smiled upon the silent sea,
And bade the frozen streams be free,
And waked to music all their fountains,
And breathed upon the frozen mountains,
And like a prophetess of May
Strewed flowers upon the barren way,
Making the wintry world appear
Like one on whom thou smilest, dear
Away, away, from men and towns,
To the wild wood and the downs –
To the silent wilderness
Where the soul need not repress
Its music lest it should not find

An echo in another's mind,
While the touch of Nature's art
Harmonizes heart to heart.
I leave this notice on my door
For each accustomed visitor:–
'I am gone into the fields
To take what this sweet hour yields;–
Reflection, you may come to-morrow,
Sit by the fireside with Sorrow.–
You with the unpaid bill, Despair,–
You, tiresome verse-reciter, Care,–
I will pay you in the grave,–
Death will listen to your stave.
Expectation too, be off!
To-day is for itself enough;
Hope, in pity mock not Woe
With smiles, nor follow where I go;
Long having lived on thy sweet food,
At length I find one moment's good
After long pain – with all your love,
That you never told me of.'

Radiant Sister of the Day,
Awake! Arise! And come away!
To the wild woods and the plains,

And the pools where winter rains
Image all their roof of leaves,
Where the pine its garland weaves
Of sapless green and ivy dun
Round stems that never kiss the sun;
Where the lawns and pastures be,
And the sandhills of the sea; –
Where the melting hoar-frost wets
The daisy-star that never sets,
And wind-flowers, and violets,
Which yet join not scent to hue,
Crown the pale year weak and new;
When the night is left behind
In the deep east, dun and blind,
And the blue noon is over us,
And the multitudinous
Billows murmur at our feet,
Where the earth and ocean meet,
And all things seem only one
In the universal sun.

Percy Bysshe Shelley (1792–1822)

Thaw

Over the land freckled with snow half-thawed
The speculating rooks at their nests cawed
And saw from elm-tops, delicate as flower of grass,
What we below could not see, Winter pass.

Edward Thomas (1878–1917)

Gratiana Dauncing and Singing

I

See! With what constant Motion
Even, and glorious, as the Sunne,
  Gratiana steers that Noble Frame,
Soft as her breast, sweet as her voyce
That gave each winding Law and poyze,
  And swifter than the wings of Fame.

II

She beat the happy Pavement
By such a Starre made Firmament,
  Which now no more the Roofe envies;
But swells up high with *Atlas* ev'n
Bearing the brighter, nobler Heav'n,
  And in her, all the Dieties.

III

Each step trod out a Lovers thought
And the Ambitious hopes he brought,
   Chain'd to her brave feet with such arts;
Such sweet command, and gentle awe,
As when she ceas'd, we sighing saw
   The floor lay pav'd with broken hearts.

IV

So did she move; so did she sing
Like the Harmonious spheres that bring
   Unto their Rounds their musick's ayd;
Which she performed such a way,
As all th'inamoured world will say:
   The *Graces* daunced, and *Apollo* play'd.

Richard Lovelace (1618–1658)

Music

The neighbour sits in his window and plays the flute.
From my bed I can hear him,
And the round notes flutter and tap about the room,
And hit against each other,
Blurring to unexpected chords.
It is very beautiful,
With the little flute-notes all about me,
In the darkness.

In the daytime,
The neighbour eats bread and onions with one hand
And copies music with the other.
He is fat and has a bald head,
So I do not look at him,
But run quickly past his window.
There is always the sky to look at,
Or the water in the well!

But when night comes and he plays his flute,
I think of him as a young man,
With gold seals hanging from his watch,
And a blue coat with silver buttons.
As I lie in my bed
The flute-notes push against my ears and lips,
And I go to sleep, dreaming.

Amy Lowell (1874–1925)

February

In February I give you gallant sport
   Of harts and hinds and great wild boars; and all
   Your company good foresters and tall,
With buskins strong, with jerkins close and short;
And in your leashes, hounds of brave report;
   And from your purses, plenteous money-fall,
   In very spleen of misers' starveling gall,
Who at your generous customs snarl and snort.
At dusk wend homeward, ye and all your folk,
   All laden from the wilds, to your carouse,
     With merriment and songs accompanied:
And so draw wine and let the kitchen smoke;
   And so be till the first watch glorious;
     Then sound sleep to you till the day be wide.

Folgóre da San Gimignano (c. 1270–c. 1332)
Translated by Dante Gabriel Rossetti (1828–1882)

Conviction

I like to get off with people,
I like to lie in their arms,
I like to be held and tightly kissed,
Safe from all alarms.

I like to laugh and be happy
With a beautiful beautiful kiss,
I tell you, in all the world
There is no bliss like this.

Stevie Smith (1902–1971)

Butterfly Laughter

In the middle of our porridge plates
There was a blue butterfly painted
And each morning we tried who should reach the
    butterfly first.
Then the Grandmother said: 'Do not eat the poor
    butterfly.'
That made us laugh.
Always she said it and always it started us laughing.
It seemed such a sweet little joke.
I was certain that one fine morning
The butterfly would fly out of our plates,
Laughing the teeniest laugh in the world,
And perch on the Grandmother's lap.

Katherine Mansfield (1888–1923)

The Winter Evening

FROM *THE TASK*, BOOK IV, LINES 36–41

Now stir the fire, and close the shutters fast,
Let fall the curtains, wheel the sofa round,
And, while the bubbling and loud-hissing urn
Throws up a steamy column, and the cups,
That cheer but not inebriate, wait on each,
So let us welcome peaceful ev'ning in.

William Cowper (1731–1800)

All Day I've Toiled But Not With Pain

All day I've toiled but not with pain
In learning's golden mine
And now at eventide again
The moonbeams softly shine

There is no snow upon the ground
No frost on wind or wave
The south wind blew with gentlest sound
And broke their icy grave

'Tis sweet to wander here at night
To watch the winter die
With heart as summer sunshine light
And warm as summer's sky

O may I never lose the peace
That lulls me gently now
Though time may change my youthful face
And years may shade my brow

True to myself and true to all
May I be healthful still
And turn away from passion's call
And curb my own wild will

Emily Brontë (1818-1848)

High Flight

Oh! I have slipped the surly bonds of earth
And danced the skies on laughter-silvered wings;
Sunward I've climbed, and joined the tumbling mirth
Of sun-split clouds, – and done a hundred things
You have not dreamed of – wheeled and soared and swung
High in the sunlit silence. Hov'ring there,
I've chased the shouting wind along, and flung
My eager craft through footless halls of air.
Up, up the long, delirious burning blue
I've topped the wind-swept heights with easy grace
Where never lark, or even eagle flew;
And, while with silent, lifting mind I've trod
The high untrespassed sanctity of space,
Put out my hand, and touched the face of God.

John Gillespie Magee Jr (1922–1941)

Roundel

FROM *THE PARLEMENT OF FOULES*

Now welcom somer, with thy sonne softe,
That hast this wintres weders over-shake,
And driven awey the longe nightes blake!

Seynt Valentyn, that art ful hy on-lofte; –
Thus singen smale foules for thy sake –
Now welcom somer, with thy sonne softe,
That hast this wintres weders over-shake.

Wel han they cause for to gladen ofte,
Sith ech of hem recovered hath his make;
Ful blisful may they singen whan they wake;
Now welcom somer, with thy sonne softe,
That hast this wintres weders over-shake,
And driven awey the longe nightes blake.

Geoffrey Chaucer (c. 1340–1400)
Edited by Walter W. Skeat (1835–1912)

On a Train

The book I've been reading
rests on my knee. You sleep.

It's beautiful out there –
fields, little lakes and winter trees
in February sunlight,
every car park a shining mosaic.

Long, radiant minutes,
your hand in my hand
still warm, still warm.

Wendy Cope (1945–)

The Policeman's Lot

FROM *THE PIRATES OF PENZANCE*

When a felon's not engaged in his employment
   Or maturing his felonious little plans,
His capacity for innocent enjoyment
   Is just as great as any honest man's
Our feelings we with difficulty smother
   When constabulary duty's to be done:
Ah, take one consideration with another,
   The policeman's lot is not a happy one.

When the enterprising burglar isn't burgling
   When the cut-throat isn't occupied in crime
He loves to hear the little brook a-gurgling,
   And listen to the merry village chime.
When the coster's finished jumping on his mother,
   He loves to lie a-basking in the sun
Ah, take one consideration with another,
   The policeman's lot is not a happy one!

W. S. Gilbert (1836–1911)

To My Dear and Loving Husband

If ever two were one, then surely we.
If ever man were loved by wife, then thee;
If ever wife was happy in a man,
Compare with me, ye women, if you can.
I prize thy love more than whole mines of gold
Or all the riches that the East doth hold.
My love is such that rivers cannot quench,
Nor ought but love from thee, give recompense.
Thy love is such I can no way repay,
The heavens reward thee manifold, I pray.
Then while we live, in love let's so persevere
That when we live no more, we may live for ever.

Anne Bradstreet (1612–1672)

In Memory of a Happy Day in February

VERSES 1–7

Blessed be Thou for all the joy
  My soul has felt to-day!
Oh, let its memory stay with me,
  And never pass away!

I was alone, for those I loved
  Were far away from me;
The sun shone on the withered grass,
  The wind blew fresh and free.

Was it the smile of early spring
  That made my bosom glow?
'Twas sweet; but neither sun nor wind
  Could cheer my spirit so.

Was it some feeling of delight
  All vague and undefined?
No; 'twas a rapture deep and strong,
  Expanding in my mind!

Was it a sanguine view of life
   And all its transient bliss –
A hope of bright prosperity?
   Oh, no! it was not this!

It was a glimpse of truths divine
   Unto my spirit given,
Illumined by a ray of light
   That shone direct from Heaven!

I felt there was a God on high
   By whom all things were made;
I saw His wisdom and His power
   In all his works displayed.

Anne Brontë (1820–1849)

The Miracle

Come, sweetheart, listen, for I have a thing
Most wonderful to tell you – news of spring.

Albeit winter still is in the air,
And the earth troubled, and the branches bare,

Yet down the fields to-day I saw her pass –
The spring – her feet went shining through the grass.

She touched the ragged hedgerows – I have seen
Her finger-prints, most delicately green;

And she has whispered to the crocus leaves,
And to the garrulous sparrows in the eaves.

Swiftly she passed and shyly, and her fair
Young face was hidden in her cloudy hair.

She would not stay, her season is not yet,
But she has reawakened, and has set

The sap of all the world astir, and rent
Once more the shadows of our discontent.

Triumphant news – a miracle I sing –
The everlasting miracle of spring.

John Drinkwater (1882–1937)

One Hour to Madness and Joy

One hour to madness and joy! O furious! O confine me
    not!
(What is this that frees me so in storms?
What do my shouts amid lightnings and raging winds
    mean?)

O to drink the mystic deliria deeper than any other man!
O savage and tender achings! (I bequeath them to you
    my children,
I tell them to you, for reasons, O bridegroom and bride.)

O to be yielded to you whoever you are, and you to be
    yielded to me in defiance of the world!
O to return to Paradise! O bashful and feminine!
O to draw you to me, to plant on you for the first time
    the lips of a determin'd man.

O the puzzle, the thrice-tied knot, the deep and dark
    pool, all untied and illumin'd!
O to speed where there is space enough and air enough
    at last!
To be absolv'd from previous ties and conventions,
    I from mine and you from yours!
To find a new unthought-of nonchalance with the best
    of Nature!
To have the gag remov'd from one's mouth!
To have the feeling to-day or any day I am sufficient as
    I am.

O something unprov'd! something in a trance!
To escape utterly from others' anchors and holds!
To drive free! to love free! to dash reckless and
   dangerous!
To court destruction with taunts, with invitations!
To ascend, to leap to the heavens of the love indicated to
   me!
To rise thither with my inebriate soul!
To be lost if it must be so!
To feed the remainder of life with one hour of fulness
   and freedom!
With one brief hour of madness and joy.

Walt Whitman (1819–1892)

Friends

FROM *THE CHOICE*, LINES 74–97

That life may be more comfortable yet,
And all my joys refined, sincere and great,
I'd choose two friends, whose company would be
A great advance to my felicity:
Well born, of humours suited to my own;
Discreet, and men as well as books, have known.
Brave, gen'rous, witty, and exactly free
From loose behaviour, or formality;
Airy and prudent, merry, but not light,
Quick in discerning, and in judging right.
Secret they should be, faithful to their trust;
In reas'ning cool, strong, temperate and just;
Obliging, open, without huffing, brave,
Brisk in gay talking, and in sober, grave;
Close in dispute, but not tenacious, tried
By solid reason, and let that decide;
Not prone to lust, revenge, or envious hate,
Nor busy meddlers with intrigues of state;
Strangers to slander, and sworn foes to spite:
Not quarrelsome, but stout enough to fight;
Loyal and pious, friends to Caesar true,
As dying martyrs to their Maker too.
In their society, I could not miss
A permanent, sincere, substantial bliss.

John Pomfret (1667–1702)

Londoner

Scarcely two hours back in the country
and I'm shopping in East Finchley High Road
in a cotton skirt, a cardigan, jandals –
or flipflops as people call them here,
where February's winter. Aren't I cold?
The neighbours in their overcoats are smiling
at my smiles and not at my bare toes:
they know me here.
                I hardly know myself,
yet. It takes me until Monday evening,
walking from the office after dark
to Westminster Bridge. It's cold, it's foggy,
the traffic's as abominable as ever,
and there across the Thames is County Hall,
that uninspired stone body, floodlit.
It makes me laugh. In fact, it makes me sing.

Fleur Adcock (1934–)

Winter Rain

Every valley drinks,
   Every dell and hollow:
Where the kind rain sinks and sinks,
   Green of Spring will follow.

Yet a lapse of weeks
   Buds will burst their edges,
Strip their wool-coats, glue-coats, streaks,
   In the woods and hedges;

Weave a bower of love
   For birds to meet each other,
Weave a canopy above
   Nest and egg and mother.

But for fattening rain
   We should have no flowers,
Never a bud or leaf again
   But for soaking showers;

Never a mated bird
  In the rocking tree-tops,
Never indeed a flock or herd
  To graze upon the lea-crops.

Lambs so woolly white,
  Sheep the sun-bright leas on,
They could have no grass to bite
  But for rain in season.

We should find no moss
  In the shadiest places,
Find no waving meadow grass
  Pied with broad-eyed daisies:

But miles of barren sand,
  With never a son or daughter,
Not a lily on the land,
  Or lily on the water.

Christina Rossetti (1830–1894)

Last Week of February, 1890

Hark to the merry birds, hark how they sing!
  Although 'tis not yet spring
    And keen the air;
Hale Winter, half resigning ere he go,
  Doth to his heiress shew
    His kingdom fair.

In patient russet is his forest spread,
  All bright with bramble red,
    With beechen moss
And holly sheen: the oak silver and stark
  Sunneth his aged bark
    And wrinkled boss.

But neath the ruin of the withered brake
  Primroses now awake
    From nursing shades:
The crumpled carpet of the dry leaves brown
  Avails not to keep down
    The hyacinth blades.

The hazel hath put forth his tassels ruffed;
    The willow's flossy tuft
        Hath slipped him free:
The rose amid her ransacked orange hips
    Braggeth the tender tips
        Of bowers to be.

A black rook stirs the branches here and there,
    Foraging to repair
        His broken home:
And hark, on the ash boughs! Never thrush did sing
    Louder in praise of spring,
        When spring is come.

Robert Bridges (1844–1930)

Joy and Pleasure

Now, Joy is born of parents poor,
　And Pleasure of our richer kind;
Though Pleasure's free, she cannot sing
　As sweet a song as Joy confined.

Pleasure's a Moth, that sleeps by day
　And dances by false glare at night;
But Joy's a Butterfly, that loves
　To spread its wings in Nature's light.

Joy's like a Bee that gently sucks
　Away on blossoms its sweet hour;
But Pleasure's like a greedy Wasp,
　That plums and cherries would devour.

Joy's like a Lark that lives alone,
　Whose ties are very strong, though few;
But Pleasure like a Cuckoo roams,
　Makes much acquaintance, no friends true.

Joy from her heart doth sing at home,
　With little care if others hear;
But Pleasure then is cold and dumb,
　And sings and laughs with strangers near.

W. H. Davies (1871–1940)

Mirth

FROM *THE KNIGHT OF THE BURNING PESTLE*

'Tis mirth that fils the veins with bloud,
More than wine, or sleep, or food.
Let each man keep his heart at ease,
No man dies of that disease.
He that would his body keep
From diseases, must not weep,
But whoever laughs and sings,
Never his body brings
Into Fevers, Gouts or Rhumes,
Or lingringly his lungs consumes:
Or meets with Aches in the bone,
Or Cathathes, or griping Stone:
But contented lives for aye;
The more he laughs, the more he may.

Francis Beaumont (1584–1616) and John Fletcher (1579–1625)

Dream-Pedlary

VERSES I AND II

If there were dreams to sell,
    What would you buy?
Some cost a passing bell;
    Some a light sigh,
That shakes from Life's fresh crown
    Only a rose-leaf down.
If there were dreams to sell,
Merry and sad to tell,
And the crier rang the bell,
    What would you buy?

A cottage lone and still,
    With bowers nigh,
Shadowy, my woes to still,
    Until I die.
Such pearl from Life's fresh crown
Fain would I shake me down.
Were dreams to have at will,
This best would heal my ill,
    This would I buy.

Thomas Lovell Beddoes (1803–1849)

The Confirmation

Yes, yours, my love, is the right human face.
I in my mind had waited for this long,
Seeing the false and searching for the true,
Then found you as a traveller finds a place
Of welcome suddenly amid the wrong
Valleys and rocks and twisting roads. But you,
What shall I call you? A fountain in a waste,
A well of water in a country dry,
Or anything that's honest and good, an eye
That makes the whole world bright. Your open heart,
Simple with giving, gives the primal deed,
The first good world, the blossom, the blowing seed,
The hearth, the steadfast land, the wandering sea,
Not beautiful or rare in every part,
But like yourself, as they were meant to be.

Edwin Muir (1887–1959)

Winter's Turning

Snow is still on the ground,
But there is a golden brightness in the air.
Across the river,
Blue,
Blue,
Sweeping widely under the arches
Of many bridges,
Is a spire and a dome,
Clear as though ringed with ice-flakes,
Golden, and pink, and jocund.
On a near-by steeple,
A golden weather-cock flashes smartly,
His open beak 'Cock-a-doodle-dooing'
Straight at the ear of Heaven.
A tall apartment house,
Crocus-coloured,
Thrusts up from the street
Like a new-sprung flower.
Another street is edged and patterned

With the bloom of bricks,
Houses and houses of rose-red bricks,
Every window a-glitter.
The city is a parterre,
Blowing and glowing,
Alight with the wind,
Washed over with gold and mercury.
Let us throw up our hats,
For we are past the age of balls
And have none handy.
Let us take hold of hands,
And race along the sidewalks,
And dodge the traffic in crowded streets.
Let us whir with the golden spoke-wheels
Of the sun.
For to-morrow Winter drops into the waste-basket,
And the calendar calls it March.

Amy Lowell (1874–1925)

MARCH

Dancing in the Breeze

The Year's at the Spring

FROM *PIPPA PASSES*

The year's at the spring,
And day's at the morn;
Morning's at seven;
The hill-side's dew-pearled;
The lark's on the wing;
The snail's on the thorn;
God's in His heaven –
All's right with the world!

Robert Browning (1812–1889)

The Merry Country Lad

FROM *THE PASSIONATE SHEPHERD*

Who can live in heart so glad
As the merry country lad?
Who upon a fair green balk
May at pleasure sit and walk,
And amid the azure skies
See the morning sun arise;
While he hears in every spring,
How the birds do chirp and sing.

Nicholas Breton (1545–1626)

Sowing

It was a perfect day
For sowing; just
As sweet and dry was the ground
As tobacco-dust.

I tasted deep the hour
Between the far
Owl's chuckling first soft cry
And the first star.

A long stretched hour it was;
Nothing undone
Remained; the early seeds
All safely sown.

And now, hark at the rain,
Windless and light,
Half a kiss, half a tear,
Saying good-night.

Edward Thomas (1878–1917)

Green Rain

Into the scented woods we'll go
And see the blackthorn swim in snow.
High above, in the budding leaves,
A brooding dove awakes and grieves;
The glades with mingled music stir,
And wildly laughs the woodpecker.
When blackthorn petals pearl the breeze,
There are the twisted hawthorn trees
Thick-set with buds, as clear and pale
As golden water or green hail –
As if a storm of rain had stood
Enchanted in the thorny wood,
And, hearing fairy voices call,
Hung poised, forgetting how to fall.

Mary Webb (1881–1927)

The Rapture

Sweet Infancy!
O Heavenly Fire! O Sacred Light!
How fair and Bright!
How Great am I
Whom all the World doth magnify!

O heavenly Joy!
O Great and Sacred Blessedness
Which I possess!
So great a Joy
Who did into my Arms convey?

From God above
Being sent, the Gift doth me enflame:
To praise his Name;
The Stars do move,
The Sun doth shine, to shew his Love.

O how Divine
Am I! To all this Sacred Wealth,
This Life and Health,
Who rais'd? Who mine
Did make the same? What hand divine?

Thomas Traherne (1636/7–1674)

Hidden Joys

Pleasures lie thickest where no pleasures seem,
There's not a leaf that falls upon the ground
But holds some joy, of silence or of sound;
Some sprite begotten of a summer dream.
The very meanest things are made supreme
With innate ecstasy. No grain of sand
But moves a bright and million-peopled land,
And hath its Edens and its Eves I deem.
For Love, though blind himself, a curious eye
Hath lent me, to behold the hearts of things,
And touched mine ear with power. Thus far or nigh,
Minute or mighty, fixed, or free with wings,
Delight from many a nameless covert sly
Peeps sparkling, and in tones familiar sings.

Samuel Laman Blanchard (1804–1845)

The Wishing Tree

I stand neither in the wilderness
nor fairyland

but in the fold
of a green hill

the tilt from one parish
into another.

To look at me
through a smirr of rain

is to taste the iron
in your own blood

because I hoard
the common currency

of longing: each wish
each secret assignation.

My limbs lift, scabbed
with greenish coins

I draw into my slow wood
fleur-de-lys, the enthroned Britannia.

Behind me, the land
reaches toward the Atlantic.

And though I'm poisoned
choking on the small change

of human hope,
daily beaten into me

look: I am still alive –
in fact, in bud.

Kathleen Jamie (1962–)

He Ate and Drank the Precious Words

He ate and drank the precious Words –
His Spirit grew robust –
He knew no more that he was poor,
Nor that his frame was Dust –

He danced along the dingy Days
And this Bequest of Wings
Was but a Book – What Liberty
A loosened spirit brings –

Emily Dickinson (1830–1886)

The Angel That Presided

The Angel that presided o'er my birth
Said 'Little creature, form'd of joy and mirth,
Go, love without the help of anything on earth.'

William Blake (1757–1827)

Come Hither

FROM *THE CAPTAIN*

Come hither, you that love, and hear me sing
    Of Joys still growing,
Green, fresh, and lusty, as the Pride of Spring,
    And ever blowing.
Come hither, Youths that blush, and dare not know
    What is Desire,
And old Men, worse than you, that cannot blow
    One Spark of Fire;
And with the Power of my enchanting Song,
Boys shall be able Men, and old Men young.

Come hither, you that hope, and you that cry,
    Leave off complaining,
Youth, Strength, and Beauty, that shall never die,
    Are here remaining.
Come hither, Fools, and blush you stay so long
    From being blest,
And mad Men, worse than you, that suffer Wrong,
    Yet seek no Rest.
And in an Hour, with my enchanting Song,
You shall be ever pleas'd, and young Maids long.

John Fletcher (1579–1625) and Francis Beaumont (1584–1616)

Song

1

After the pangs of a desperate Lover,
When day and night I have sigh'd all in vain,
Ah what pleasure it is to discover
In her eyes pity, who causes my pain!

2

When with unkindness our love at a stand is,
And both have punish'd ourselves with pain,
Ah what a pleasure the touch of her hand is,
Ah what a pleasure to press it again!

3

When the denyal comes fainter and fainter,
And her eyes give what her tongue does deny,
Ah what a trembling I feel when I venture,
Ah what a trembling does usher my joy!

4

When, with a Sigh, she accords me the blessing,
And her eyes twinkle 'twixt pleasure and pain,
Ah what a joy 'tis beyond all expressing,
Ah what a joy to hear, shall we again!

John Dryden (1631–1700)

I Wandered Lonely as a Cloud

WRITTEN AT TOWN-END, GRASMERE

I wandered lonely as a cloud
That floats on high o'er vales and hills,
When all at once I saw a crowd,
A host, of golden daffodils;
Beside the lake, beneath the trees,
Fluttering and dancing in the breeze.

Continuous as the stars that shine
And twinkle on the milky way,
They stretched in never-ending line
Along the margin of the bay:
Ten thousand saw I at a glance,
Tossing their heads in sprightly dance.

The waves beside them danced; but they
Out-did the sparkling waves in glee:
A poet could not but be gay,
In such a jocund company:
I gazed – and gazed – but little thought
What wealth the show to me had brought:

For oft, when on my couch I lie
In vacant or in pensive mood,
They flash upon that inward eye
Which is the bliss of solitude;
And then my heart with pleasure fills,
And dances with the daffodils.

William Wordsworth (1770–1850)

After the Examination

When someone's happy in a house there shows
A chink of honey-coloured light beneath the bedroom
  door,
Where once a thunder-purple gloom oozed out across
  the floor;
And even the stairs smell like an early rose.

Frances Cornford (1886–1960)

The Idle Life I Lead

The idle life I lead
Is like a pleasant sleep,
Wherein I rest and heed
The dreams that by me sweep

And still of all my dreams
In turn so swiftly past,
Each in its fancy seems
A nobler than the last.

And every eve I say,
Noting my step in bliss,
That I have known no day
In all my life like this.

Robert Bridges (1844–1930)

Love's Matrimony

There is no happier life
But in a wife,
The comforts are so sweet
When two do meet:
'Tis plenty, peace, a calm
Like dropping balm;
Love's weather is so fair,
Like perfumèd air;
Each word such pleasure brings
Like soft-touched stirrings;
Love's passion moves the heart
On either part.
Such harmony together,
So pleased in either,
No discords, concords still,
Sealed with one will.
By love, God made man one,
Yet not alone:
Like stamps of king and queen
It may be seen,
Two figures on one coin;
So do they join,
Only they not embrace,
We face to face.

William Cavendish (1592–1676)

Delight of Being Alone

I know no greater delight than the sheer delight of being
   alone.
It makes me realise the delicious pleasure of the moon
that she has in travelling by herself: throughout time,
or the splendid growing of an ash-tree
alone, on a hillside in the north, humming in the wind.

D. H. Lawrence (1885–1930)

Song of the Open Road

LINES 1–7

Afoot and light-hearted, I take to the open road,
Healthy, free, the world before me,
The long brown path before me, leading wherever
   I choose.

Henceforth I ask not good-fortune – I myself am
   good-fortune,
Henceforth I whimper no more, postpone no more,
   need nothing,
Done with indoor complaints, libraries, querulous
   criticisms,
Strong and content I travel the open road.

Walt Whitman (1819–1892)

March

In March I give you plenteous fisheries
   Of lamprey and of salmon, eel and trout,
   Dental and dolphin, sturgeon, all the rout
Of fish in all the streams that fill the seas.
With fishermen and fishing-boats at ease,
   Sail-barques and arrow-barques, and galleons stout,
   To bear you, while the season lasts, far out,
And back, through spring, to any port you please.
But with fair mansions see that it be fill'd,
   With everything exactly to your mind,
     And every sort of comfortable folk.
No convent suffer there, nor priestly guild:
   Leave the mad monks to preach after their kind
     Their scanty truth, their lies beyond a joke.

Folgóre da San Gimignano (c. 1270–c. 1332)
Translated by Dante Gabriel Rossetti (1828–1882)

Song

FROM *THE GYPSIES METAMORPHOSED*

The fairy beam upon you,
The stars to glister on you:
    A moon of light,
    In the noon of night
Till the fire-drake hath o'ergone you.

The wheel of fortune guide you,
The boy with the bow beside you
    Run aye in the way
    Till the bird of day,
And the luckier lot betide you.

Ben Jonson (1572–1637)

A Morning Song

(FOR THE FIRST DAY OF SPRING)

Morning has broken
Like the first morning
Blackbird has spoken
    Like the first bird.
Praise for the singing!
Praise for the morning!
Praise for them springing
  From the first Word.

Sweet the rain's new fall,
Sunlit from heaven
Like the first dew fall
    In the first hour.
Praise for the sweetness
Of the wet garden
Sprung in completeness
  From the first shower.

Mine is the sunlight!
Mine is the morning!
Born of the one light
  Eden saw play.
Praise with elation,
Praise every morning
Spring's recreation
  Of the First Day!

Eleanor Farjeon (1881–1965)

To Ianthe

FROM *CHILDE HAROLD'S PILGRIMAGE*, VERSES I AND II

Not in those climes where I have late been straying,
Though Beauty long hath there been matchless deem'd;
Not in those visions to the heart displaying
Forms which it sighs but to have only dream'd,
Hath aught like thee in truth or fancy seem'd:
Nor, having seen thee, shall I vainly seek
To paint those charms which varied as they beam'd –
To such as see thee not my words were weak;
To those who gaze on thee what language could they speak?

Ah! may'st thou ever be what now thou art,
Nor unbeseem the promise of thy spring,
As fair in form, as warm yet pure in heart,
Love's image upon earth without his wing,
And guileless beyond Hope's imagining!
And surely she who now so fondly rears
Thy youth, in thee, thus hourly brightening,
Beholds the rainbow of her future years,
Before whose heavenly hues all sorrow disappears.

George Gordon, Lord Byron (1788–1824)

There is Pleasure in the Wet, Wet Clay

There is pleasure in the wet, wet clay,
When the artist's hand is potting it.
There is pleasure in the wet, wet lay,
When the poet's pad is blotting it.
There is pleasure in the shine of your picture on the line
At the Royal Academy;
But the pleasure felt in these is as chalk to Cheddar cheese
When it comes to a well made Lie. –
To a quite unwreckable Lie,
To a most impeccable Lie!
To a water-tight, fire-proof, angle-iron, sunk-hinge,
    time-lock, steel-faced Lie!
Not a private hansom Lie,
But a pair-and-brougham Lie,
Not a little-place-at-Tooting, but a country-house-with-
    shooting
And a ring-fence-deer-park Lie.

Rudyard Kipling (1865–1936)

In the Fields

Lord, when I look at lovely things which pass,
    Under old trees the shadows of young leaves
Dancing to please the wind along the grass,
    Or the gold stillness of the August sun on the
      August sheaves;
Can I believe there is a heavenlier world than this?
    And if there is
Will the strange heart of any everlasting thing
    Bring me these dreams that take my breath away?
They come at evening with the home-flying rooks and the
  scent of hay,
    Over the fields they come. They come in Spring.

Charlotte Mew (1869–1928)

Music

When music sounds, gone is the earth I know,
And all her lovely things even lovelier grow;
Her flowers in vision flame, her forest trees
Lift burdened branches, stilled with ecstasies.

When music sounds, out of the water rise
Naiads whose beauty dims my waking eyes,
Rapt in strange dreams burns each enchanted face,
With solemn echoing stirs their dwelling-place.

When music sounds, all that I was I am
Ere to this haunt of brooding dust I came;
When from Time's woods break into distant song
The swift-winged hours, as I hasten along.

Walter de la Mare (1873–1956)

The Wish

Well then! I now do plainly see
This busy world and I shall ne'er agree.
The very honey of all earthly joy
Does of all meats the soonest cloy;
    And they, methinks, deserve my pity
Who for it can endure the stings,
The crowd, and buzz, and murmurings,
Of this great hive, the city.

Ah, yet, ere I descend to the grave
May I a small house and large garden have;
And a few friends, and many books, both true,
Both wise, and both delightful too!
And since love ne'er will from me flee,
A Mistress moderately fair,
And good as guardian angels are,
Only beloved and loving me.

O fountains! when in you shall I
Myself eased of unpeaceful thoughts espy?
O fields! O woods! when, when shall I be made
Thy happy tenant of your shade?
Here's the spring-head of Pleasure's flood:
Here's wealthy Nature's treasury,
Where all the riches lie that she
Has coin'd and stamp'd for good.

Pride and ambition here
Only in far-fetch'd metaphors appear;
Here nought but winds can hurtful murmurs scatter,
And nought but Echo flatter.
The gods, when they descended, hither
From heaven did always choose their way:
And therefore we may boldly say
That 'tis the way too thither.

How happy here should I
And one dear She live, and embracing die!
She who is all the world, and can exclude
In deserts solitude.
I should have then this only fear:
Lest men, when they my pleasures see,
Should hither throng to live like me,
And so make a city here.

Abraham Cowley (1618–1667)

Coffee

When the sweet Poison of the Treacherous Grape
Had acted on the world a general rape;
Drowning our Reason and our souls
In such deep seas of large o'erflowing bowls,

When foggy Ale, leavying up mighty trains
Of muddy vapours, had besieg'd our brains,
Then Heaven in Pity ...
First sent amongst us this All-healing Berry.

Coffee arrives, that grave and wholesome Liquor,
That heals the stomach, makes the genius quicker,
Relieves the memory, revives the sad,
And cheers the Spirits, without making mad ...

Anon, published 1674

Photographs

At twelve I didn't like my own face, because
my eyes were huge and open as a dog's,
and I wanted slitty eyes like Virginia Mayo.

Photographs show me laughing and healthy,
with wide shoulders and strong wrists that could take me
up the pear tree to the highest boughs.

Between these brown card covers adolescence
stirs. 'Oh Daddy,' I asked once
'why aren't I prettier?' He was kindly but embarrassed.

Now I look back on photographs of that girl
as if I were already some ginger-haired ghost
visiting a sepia world of strangers,

and among so many faces I like most
her laughter lines, strong nose and windblown hair.
And if I could fly back I should whisper to her

where she stands, painted and scared in the dance hall
setting out her sexual wares: What you
think of as disadvantages will bring you through.

Elaine Feinstein (1930–2019)

Early Morning Song

Nothing fairer than the light
On petals opening, gold and white,
To the morning, to the blue,
In a world of song and dew.

Nothing fairer than two eyes
That behold with shy surprise
The miracle that no man can stay –
Darkness turning into day.

Rachel Field (1894–1942)

The Tables Turned

VERSES I–V

Up! up! my Friend, and quit your books;
Or surely you'll grow double:
Up! up! my Friend, and clear your looks;
Why all this toil and trouble?

The sun above the mountain's head,
A freshening lustre mellow
Through all the long green fields has spread,
His first sweet evening yellow.

Books! 'tis a dull and endless strife:
Come, hear the woodland linnet,
How sweet his music! on my life,
There's more of wisdom in it.

And hark! how blithe the throstle sings!
He, too, is no mean preacher:
Come forth into the light of things,
Let Nature be your teacher.

She has a world of ready wealth,
Our minds and hearts to bless –
Spontaneous wisdom breathed by health,
Truth breathed by cheerfulness.

William Wordsworth (1770–1850)

A Pipe of Tobacco

IMITATION II

Tenues fugit ceu fumus in auras. Virg.

Little tube of mighty pow'r,
Charmer of an idle hour,
Object of my warm desire,
Lip of wax and eye of fire:
And thy snowy taper waist,
With my finger gently brac'd;
And thy pretty swelling crest,
With my little stopper prest,
And the sweetest bliss of blisses,
Breathing from thy balmy kisses,
Happy thrice and thrice agen,
Happiest he of happy men;
Who when agen the night returns,
When agen the taper burns;
When agen the cricket's gay
(Little cricket, full of play)
Can afford his tube to feed,
With the fragrant INDIAN weed;
Pleasure for a nose divine,
Incense of the god of wine.
Happy thrice and thrice agen,
Happiest he of happy men.

Isaac Hawkins Browne (1705–1760)

New Every Morning

Every morn is the world made new.
You who are weary of sorrow and sinning,
Here is a beautiful hope for you, –
A hope for me and a hope for you.

All the past things are past and over;
The tasks are done and the tears are shed.
Yesterday's errors let yesterday cover;
Yesterday's wounds, which smarted and bled,
Are healed with the healing which night has shed.

Yesterday now is a part of forever,
Bound up in a sheaf, which God holds tight,
With glad days, and sad days, and bad days, which never
Shall visit us more with their bloom and their blight,
Their fulness of sunshine or sorrowful night.

Let them go, since we cannot re-live them,
Cannot undo and cannot atone;
God in his mercy receive, forgive them!
Only the new days are our own;
To-day is ours, and to-day alone.

Here are the skies all burnished brightly,
Here is the spent earth all re-born,
Here are the tired limbs springing lightly
To face the sun and to share with the morn
In the chrism of dew and the cool of dawn.

Every day is a fresh beginning;
Listen, my soul, to the glad refrain,
And, spite of old sorrow and older sinning,
And puzzles forecasted and possible pain,
Take heart with the day, and begin again.

Susan Coolidge (1835–1905)

APRIL

Blessing in the Air

The Crow

With rakish eye and plenished crop,
  Oblivious of the farmer's gun,
Upon the naked ash-tree top
  The Crow sits basking in the sun.

An old ungodly rogue, I wot!
  For, perched in black against the blue,
His feathers, torn with beak and shot,
  Let woful glints of April through.

The year's new grass, and, golden-eyed,
  The daisies sparkle underneath,
And chestnut-trees on either side
  Have opened every ruddy sheath.

But doubtful still of frost and snow,
  The ash alone stands stark and bare,
And on its topmost twig the Crow
  Takes the glad morning's sun and air.

William Canton (1845–1926)

Cats

Cats sleep,
Anywhere,
Any table,
Any chair,
Top of piano,
Window-ledge,
In the middle,
On the edge,
Open drawer,
Empty shoe,
Anybody's
Lap will do,
Fitted in a
Cardboard box,
In the cupboard,
With your frocks –
Anywhere!
They don't care!
Cats sleep
Anywhere.

Eleanor Farjeon (1881–1965)

In Memoriam

CXV

Now fades the last long streak of snow,
　Now burgeons every maze of quick
　About the flowering squares, and thick
By ashen roots the violets blow.

Now rings the woodland loud and long,
　The distance takes a lovelier hue,
　And drown'd in yonder living blue
The lark becomes a sightless song.

Now dance the lights on lawn and lea,
　The flocks are whiter down the vale,
　And milkier every milky sail
On winding stream or distant sea;

Where now the seamew pipes, or dives
　In yonder greening gleam, and fly
　The happy birds, that change their sky
To build and brood; that live their lives

From land to land; and in my breast
　Spring wakens too; and my regret
　Becomes an April violet,
And buds and blossoms like the rest.

Alfred, Lord Tennyson (1809–1892)

The Happy Life

No silks have I, no furs nor feathers,
But one old gown that knows all weathers;
No veils nor parasols nor lace,
But rough hands and a tanned face.
Yet the soft, crinkled leaves are mine
Where pale, mysterious veins shine,
And laced larches upon the blue,
And grey veils where the moon looks through;
The cries of birds across the lawns
In dark and teeming April dawns;
The sound of wings at the door-sill,
Where grows the wet-eyed tormentil;
The ripe berry's witcheries –
Its perfect round that satisfies;
And the gay scent of the wood I burn,
And the slap of butter in a busy churn.

Mary Webb (1881–1927)

The Happy Bird

The happy white throat on the sweeing bough,
Swayed by the impulse of the gadding wind
That ushers in the showers of april – now
Singeth right joyously and now reclined
Croucheth and clingeth to her moving seat
To keep her hold – and till the wind for rest
Pauses – she mutters inward melodys
That seem her hearts rich thinkings to repeat
But when the branch is still – her little breast
Swells out in raptures gushing symphonys
And then against her blown wing softly prest,
The wind comes playing an enraptured guest
This way and that she swees – till gusts arise
More boisterous in their play – then off she flies.

John Clare (1793–1864)

It Was a Lover and his Lass

FROM *AS YOU LIKE IT,* ACT V, SCENE III

It was a lover and his lass,
   With a hey, and a ho, and a hey-nonny-no,
That o'er the green cornfield did pass,
   In spring-time, the only pretty ring-time,
When birds do sing, hey ding-a-ding ding;
Sweet lovers love the spring.

Between the acres of the rye,
   With a hey, and a ho, and a hey-nonny-no,
Those pretty country folks would lie,
   In spring-time, the only pretty ring-time,
When birds do sing, hey ding-a-ding ding;
Sweet lovers love the spring.

This carol they began that hour,
   With a hey, and a ho, and a hey-nonny-no,
How that a life was but a flower
   In spring-time, the only pretty ring-time,
When birds do sing, hey ding-a-ding ding;
Sweet lovers love the spring.

And therefore take the present time,
   With a hey, and a ho, and a hey-nonny-no,
For love is crownèd with the prime
   In spring-time, the only pretty ring-time,
When birds do sing, hey ding-a-ding ding;
Sweet lovers love the spring.

William Shakespeare (1564–1616)

Chamber Music: VIII

Who goes amid the green wood
  With springtide all adorning her?
Who goes amid the merry green wood
  To make it merrier?

Who passes in the sunlight
  By ways that know the light footfall?
Who passes in the sweet sunlight
  With mien so virginal?

The ways of all the woodland
  Gleam with a soft and golden fire –
For whom does all the sunny woodland
  Carry so brave attire?

O, it is for my true love
  The woods their rich apparel wear –
O, it is for my own true love,
  That is so young and fair.

James Joyce (1882–1941)

An Odd Conceit

Lovely kind, and kindly loving,
Such a mind were worth the moving;
Truly fair, and fairly true,
Where are all these, but in you?

Wisely kind, and kindly wise;
Blessed life, where such love lies!
Wise, and kind, and fair, and true,
Lovely live all these in you.

Sweetly dear, and dearly sweet,
Blessed, where these blessings meet!
Sweet, fair, wise, kind, blessed, true,
Blessed be all these in you!

Nicholas Breton (1545–1626)

Impressions de Voyage

The sea was sapphire coloured, and the sky
　　Burned like a heated opal through air,
　　We hoisted sail; the wind was blowing fair
For the blue lands that to the Eastward lie.
From the steep prow I marked with quickening eye
　　Zakynthos, every olive grove and creek,
　　Ithaca's cliff, Lycaon's snowy peak,
And all the flower-strewn hills of Arcady.
The flapping of the sail against the mast,
　　The ripple of the water on the side,
　　The ripple of girls' laughter at the stern,
The only sounds: – when 'gan the West to burn,
　　And a red sun upon the seas to ride,
　　I stood upon the soil of Greece at last!

Oscar Wilde (1854–1900)

April Rise

If ever I saw blessing in the air
  I see it now in this still early day
Where lemon-green the vaporous morning drips
  Wet sunlight on the powder of my eye.

Blown bubble-film of blue, the sky wraps round
  Weeds of warm light whose every root and rod
Splutters with soapy green, and all the world
  Sweats with the bead of summer in its bud.

If ever I heard blessing it is there
  Where birds in trees that shoals and shadows are
Splash with their hidden wings and drops of sound
  Break on my ears their crests of throbbing air.

Pure in the haze the emerald sun dilates,
  The lips of sparrows milk the mossy stones,
While white as water by the lake a girl
  Swims her green hand among the gathered swans.

Now, as the almond burns its smoking wick,
  Dropping small flames to light the candled grass;
Now, as my low blood scales its second chance,
  If ever world were blessed, now it is.

Laurie Lee (1914–1997)

To Althea, from Prison

When love with unconfinèd wings
   Hovers within my gates,
And my divine Althea brings
   To whisper at the grates;
When I lie tangled in her hair,
   And fettered to her eye,
The gods that wanton in the air,
   Know no such liberty.

When flowing cups run swiftly round
   With no allaying Thames,
Our careless heads with roses bound,
   Our hearts with loyal flames;
When thirsty grief in wine we steep,
   When healths and draughts go free,
Fishes that tipple in the deep
   Know no such liberty.

When, like committed linnets, I
    With shriller throat shall sing
The sweetness, mercy, majesty,
    And glories of my king;
When I shall voice aloud how good
    He is, how great should be,
Enlargèd winds, that curl the flood,
    Know no such liberty.

Stone walls do not a prison make,
    Nor iron bars a cage;
Minds innocent and quiet take
    That for an hermitage:
If I have freedom in my love,
    And in my soul am free,
Angels alone that soar above,
    Enjoy such liberty.

Richard Lovelace (1617–1657)

April

The sweetest thing, I thought
At one time, between earth and heaven
Was the first smile
When mist has been forgiven
And the sun has stolen out,
Peered, and resolved to shine at seven
On dabbled lengthening grasses,
Thick primroses and early leaves uneven,
When earth's breath, warm and humid, far surpasses
The richest oven's, and loudly rings 'cuckoo'
And sharply the nightingale's 'tsoo, tsoo, tsoo, tsoo':
To say 'God bless I' was all that I could do.

But now I know one sweeter
By far since the day Emily
Turned weeping back
To me, still happy me,
To ask forgiveness, –
Yet smiled with half a certainty
To be forgiven, – for what
She had never done; I knew not what it might be,
Nor could she tell me, having now forgot,
By rapture carried with me past all care
As to an isle in April lovelier
Than April's self. 'God bless you' I said to her.

Edward Thomas (1878–1917)

Dancing on the Hill-tops

Dancing on the hill-tops,
  Singing in the valleys,
Laughing with the echoes,
  Merry little Alice.

Playing games with lambkins
  In the flowering valleys,
Gathering pretty posies,
  Helpful little Alice.

If her father's cottage
  Turned into a palace,
And he owned the hill-tops
    And the flowering valleys,
She'd be none the happier,
  Happy little Alice.

Christina Rossetti (1830–1894)

April

I give you meadow-lands in April, fair
  With over-growth of beautiful green grass;
  There among fountains the glad hours shall pass,
And pleasant ladies bring you solace there.
With steeds of Spain and ambling palfreys rare;
  Provençal songs and dances that surpass;
  And quaint French mummings; and through hollow brass
A sound of German music on the air.
And gardens ye shall have, that every one
  May lie at ease about the fragrant place;
    And each with fitting reverence shall bow down
    Unto that youth to whom I gave a crown
  Of precious jewels like to those that grace
The Babylonian Kaiser, Prester John.

Folgóre da San Gimignano (c. 1270–c. 1332)
Translated by Dante Gabriel Rossetti (1828–1882)

The Anglers Wish

I in these flowry Meads wou'd be:
These Chrystal streams should solace me:
To whose harmonious bubling noise,
I with my Angle wo'd rejoice
Sit here and see the *Turtle-Dove,*
Court his chaste Mate to acts of love,
Or on that bank, feel the west wind
Breath health and plenty, please my mind
To see sweet dew-drops kiss these flowers,
And then, washt off by *April*-showers:
Here hear my *Kenna* sing a song,
There see a Black-bird feed her young,
Or a *Leverock* build her nest;
Here, give my weary spirits rest,
And raise my low pitcht thoughts above
Earth, or what poor mortals love:
    Thus free from *Law-suits,* and the noise
    Of Princes Courts I wou'd rejoyce.

Or with my *Bryan,* and a book,
Loyter long days near *Shawford-brook;*
There sit by him, and eat my meat,
There see the Sun both rise and set:
There bid good morning to next day,
There meditate my time away:
    And angle on, and beg to have
    A quiet passage to a welcome grave.

Izaak Walton (1593–1683)

Home Thoughts from Abroad

I

Oh, to be in England
Now that April's there,
And whoever wakes in England
Sees, some morning, unaware,
That the lowest boughs and brushwood sheaf
Round the elm-tree bole are in tiny leaf,
While the chaffinch sings on the orchard bough
In England – now!

II

And after April, when May follows,
And the whitethroat builds, and all the swallows!
Hark, where my blossomed pear-tree in the hedge
Leans to the field and scatters on the clover
Blossoms and dewdrops – at the bent spray's edge –
That's the wise thrush; he sings each song twice over,
Lest you should think he never could recapture
The first fine careless rapture!
And though the fields look rough with hoary dew
All will be gay when noontide wakes anew
The buttercups, the little children's dower
 – Far brighter than this gaudy melon-flower!

Robert Browning (1812–1889)

House of Dreams

You took my empty dreams
   And filled them every one
With tenderness and nobleness,
   April and the sun.

The old empty dreams
   Where my thoughts would throng
Are far too full of happiness
   To even hold a song.

Oh, the empty dreams were dim
   And the empty dreams were wide,
They were sweet and shadowy houses
   Where my thoughts could hide.

But you took my dreams away
   And you made them all come true –
My thoughts have no place now to play,
   And nothing now to do.

Sara Teasdale (1884–1933)

The Spring

VERSES I AND II

When wintry weather's all a-done,
An' brooks do sparkle in the zun,
An' naisy-builden rooks do vlee
Wi' sticks toward their elem tree;
When birds do zing, an' we can zee
  Upon the boughs the buds o' spring, –
  Then I'm as happy as a king,
    A-vield wi' health an' zunsheen.

Vor then the cowlsip's hangen flow'r
A-wetted in the zunny show'r,
Do grow wi' vi'lets, sweet o' smell,
Bezide the wood-screen'd grægle's bell;
Where drushes' aggs, wi' sky-blue shell,
  Do lie in mossy nest among
  The thorns, while they do zing their zong
    At evenen in the zunsheen.

William Barnes (1801–1886)

At Morning on the Garden Seat

At morning on the garden seat
I dearly love to drink and eat,
To drink and eat, to drink and sing,
At morning in the time of Spring.
In winter honest men retire
And sup their possets by the fire,
And when the spring comes round again, you see,
The garden breakfast pleases me.
The morning star that melts on high
The fires that cleanse the changing sky,
The air that smells so new and sweet,
All put me in the cue to eat
A pot at five, a crust at four,
At half past six a pottle more.

Robert Louis Stevenson (1850–1894)

Green

The dawn was apple-green,
    The sky was green wine held up in the sun,
The moon was a golden petal between.

She opened her eyes, and green
    They shone, clear like flowers undone
For the first time, now for the first time seen.

ICKING

D. H. Lawrence (1885–1930)

A Frugal Plenty

FROM *THE CHOICE*, LINES 43–58

A frugal plenty should my table spread,
With healthy, not luxurious dishes fed:
Enough to satisfy, and something more
To feed the stranger and the neighb'ring poor.
Strong meat indulges vice, and pampering food
Creates diseases and inflames the blood.
But what's sufficient to make nature strong
And the bright lamp of life continue long
   I'd freely take, and as I did possess,
The bounteous Author of my plenty bless.
I'd have a little vault, but always stored
With the best wines each vintage could afford.
Wine whets the wit, improves its native force,
And gives a pleasant flavour to discourse:
By making all our spirits debonair
Throws off the lees, the sediment of care.

John Pomfret (1667–1702)

There Was Such Beauty

There was such beauty in the dappled valley
As hurt the sight, as stabbed the heart to tears
The gathered loveliness of all the years
Hovered thereover, it seemed, eternally
Set for men's Joy. Town, tower, trees, river
Under a royal azure sky for ever
Up piled with snowy towering bulks of cloud
A herald-day of Spring more wonderful
Than her true own. Trumpets cried aloud
In sky, earth, blood; no beast, no clod so dull
But of the day, and of the giver
Was glad for life, humble at once and proud.
Kyrie Eleison, and Gloria,
Credo, Jubilate, Magnificat
The whole world gathered strength to praise the day.

Ivor Gurney (1890–1937)

Look Overhead

FROM *THE BLESSED VIRGIN COMPARED TO THE
AIR WE BREATHE*, LINES 73–93

Again, look overhead
How air is azurèd;
O how! nay do but stand
Where you can lift your hand
Skywards: rich, rich it laps
Round the four fingergaps.
Yet such a sapphire-shot,
Charged, steepèd sky will not
Stain light. Yea, mark you this:
It does no prejudice.
The glass-blue days are those
When every colour glows,
Each shape and shadow shows.
Blue be it: this blue heaven
The seven or seven times seven
Hued sunbeam will transmit
Perfect, not alter it.
Or if there does some soft,
On things aloof, aloft,
Bloom breathe, that one breath more
Earth is the fairer for.

Gerard Manley Hopkins (1844–1889)

The House

There is no architect
  Can build as the Muse can;
She is skilful to select
  Materials for her plan;

Slow and warily to choose
  Rafters of immortal pine,
Or cedar incorruptible,
  Worthy her design,

She threads dark Alpine forests
  Or valleys by the sea,
In many lands, with painful steps,
  Ere she can find a tree.

She ransacks mines and ledges
  And quarries every rock,
To hew the famous adamant
  For each eternal block.

She lays her beams in music,
  In music every one,
To the cadence of the whirling world
  Which dances round the sun;

That so they shall not be displaced
  By lapses or by wars,
But for the love of happy souls
  Outlive the newest stars.

Ralph Waldo Emerson (1803–1882)

The Loveliest of Trees

A SHROPSHIRE LAD II

Loveliest of trees, the cherry now
Is hung with bloom along the bough,
And stands about the woodlands ride
Wearing white for Eastertide.

Now, of my threescore years and ten,
Twenty will not come again,
And take from seventy springs a score,
It only leaves me fifty more.

And since to look at things in bloom
Fifty springs are little room,
About the woodlands I will go
To see the cherry hung with snow.

A. E. Housman (1859–1936)

Sonnet LXXII

FROM *AMORETTI*

Oft when my spirit doth spred her bolder winges,
  In mind to mount up to the purest sky:
  it down is weighd with thoght of earthly things
  and clogd with burden of mortality,
Where when that soverayne beauty it doth spy,
  resembling heavens glory in her light:
  drawne with sweet pleasures bayt, it back doth fly,
  and unto heaven forgets her former flight.
There my fraile fancy fed with full delight,
  doth bath in blisse and mantleth most at ease:
  ne thinks of other heaven, but how it might
  her harts desire with most contentment please,
Hart need not with none other happinesse,
  but here on earth to have such hevens blisse.

Edmund Spenser (c. 1552–1599)

The Surprise

Shot from the zenith of desire
　　Some faultless beams found where I lay,
Not much expecting such white fire
　Across a slow close working-day.

What a great song then sang the brook,
　The fallen pillar's grace how new,
The vast white oaks like cowslips shook –
　And I was winged, and flew to you.

Edmund Blunden (1896–1974)

A Happy Life

O what a life is this I lead,
Far from the hum of human greed;
Where Crows, like merchants dressed in black,
Go leisurely to work and back;
Where Swallows leap and dive and float,
And Cuckoo sounds his cheerful note;
Where Skylarks now in clouds do rave,
Half mad with fret that their souls have
By hundreds far more joyous notes
Than they can manage with their throats.
The ploughman's heavy horses run
The field as if in fright – for fun,
Or stand and laugh in voices shrill;
Or roll upon their backs until
The sky's kicked small enough – they think;
Then to a pool they go and drink.
The kine are chewing their old cud,
Dreaming, and never think to add
Fresh matter that will taste – as they
Lie motionless, and dream away.

I hear the sheep a-coughing near;
Like little children, when they hear
Their elders' sympathy – so these
Sheep force their coughs on me, and please;
And many a pretty lamb I see,
Who stops his play on seeing me,
And runs and tells his mother then.
Lord, who would live in towns with men,
And hear the hum of human greed –
With such a life as this to lead?

W. H. Davies (1871–1940)

My Bed is a Boat

My bed is like a little boat;
　　Nurse helps me in when I embark;
She girds me in my sailor's coat
　　And starts me in the dark.

At night I go on board and say
　　Good-night to all my friends on shore;
I shut my eyes and sail away
　　And see and hear no more.

And sometimes things to bed I take,
　　As prudent sailors have to do;
Perhaps a slice of wedding-cake,
　　Perhaps a toy or two.

All night across the dark we steer;
　　But when the day returns at last,
Safe in my room beside the pier,
　　I find my vessel fast.

Robert Louis Stevenson (1850–1894)

Summum Bonum

FROM *ASOLANDO*

All the breath and the bloom of the year in the bag of
    one bee:
    All the wonder and wealth of the mine in the heart of
    one gem:
In the core of one pearl all the shade and the shine of the
    sea:
    Breath and bloom, shade and shine, – wonder, wealth,
    and – how far above them –
    Truth, that's brighter than gem,
    Trust, that's purer than pearl, –
Brightest truth, purest trust in the universe – all were
    for me
    In the kiss of one girl.

Robert Browning (1812–1889)

MAY

The Country of Young Laughter

Song on May Morning

Now the bright morning star, Day's harbinger,
Comes dancing from the east, and leads with her
The flowery May, who from her green lap throws
The yellow cowslip, and the pale primrose.
  Hail bounteous May, that dost inspire
  Mirth, and youth, and warm desire!
  Woods and groves are of thy dressing,
Hill and Dale, doth boast thy blessing.
Thus we salute thee with our early song,
And welcome thee, and wish thee long.

John Milton (1608–1674)

May

I give you horses for your games in May,
  And all of them well trained unto the course, –
  Each docile, swift, erect, a goodly horse;
With armour on their chests, and bells at play
Between their brows, and pennons fair and gay;
  Fine nets, and housings meet for warriors,
  Emblazoned with the shields ye claim for yours;
Gules, argent, or, all dizzy at noonday.
And spears shall split, and fruit go flying up
In merry counterchange for wreaths that drop
  From balconies and casements far above;
And tender damsels with young men and youths
Shall kiss together on the cheeks and mouths;
  And every day be glad with joyful love.

Folgóre da San Gimignano (c. 1270–c. 1332)
Translated by Dante Gabriel Rossetti (1828–1882)

Laughter

FROM *THE SPRING OF JOY*

> 'Come live, and be merry, and join with me,
>   To sing the sweet chorus of "Ha, ha, he!"'
>   William Blake

There is a path that leads from every one's door into the country of young laughter: but you must stoop to find it. The branches laugh and sigh above; willow-herb and traveller's joy cover you with their soft fleeces; fennel and flowering mint make the air spicy; the burdock and the bedstraw stretch out their hands to catch you. There the birds sit so erectly prim and so silently mirthful that you often have to clap your hand over your mouth like a child in case your echoing laughter should disturb the place. When you have gone a little way, the path may end without warning in a rabbit burrow, or the dome of a mole's winter palace, or the hanging cradle of a long-tailed tit. Then back you must go and begin again, only to come to a standstill soon before the frail barrier of a spider's web, swung from opposite thorn trees. Nothing must be broken here, or you find yourself left in a grey world, with all the irresponsible gaiety of the enchanted pathway folded in stiff sadness like a dead moth's wing.

Mary Webb (1881–1927)

The Cricketing Versions

(FOR SIMON RAE)

'There isn't much cricket in the Cromwell play.'
(overheard at a dinner party)

There isn't much cricket in Hamlet either,
There isn't much cricket in Lear.
I don't think there's any in Paradise Lost* –
I haven't a copy right here.

But I like to imagine the cricketing versions –
Laertes goes out to bat
And instead of claiming a palpable hit,
The prince gives a cry of 'Howzat!'

While elsewhere the nastier daughters of Lear
(Both women cricketers) scheme
To keep their talented younger sister
Out of the England team,

And up in the happy realms of light
When Satan is out (great catch)
His team and the winners sit down together
For sandwiches after the match.

Although there are some English writers
Who feature the red leather ball,
You could make a long list of the players and the books
In which there's no cricket at all.

To be perfectly honest, I like them that way –
The absence of cricket is fine.
But if you prefer work that includes it, please note
That now there's some cricket in mine.

*Apparently there is. 'Chaos umpire sits,/And by
decision more embroils the fray.'
Paradise Lost, Book II, lines 907–8

Wendy Cope (1945–)

Paris in Spring

The city's all a-shining
  Beneath a fickle sun,
A gay young wind's a-blowing,
  The little shower is done.
But the rain-drops still are clinging
  And falling one by one –
Oh it's Paris, it's Paris,
  And spring-time has begun.

I know the Bois is twinkling
  In a sort of hazy sheen,
And down the Champs the gray old arch
  Stands cold and still between.
But the walk is flecked with sunlight
  Where the great acacias lean,
Oh it's Paris, it's Paris,
  And the leaves are growing green.

The sun's gone in, the sparkle's dead,
  There falls a dash of rain,
But who would care when such an air
  Comes blowing up the Seine?
And still Ninette sits sewing
  Beside her window-pane,
When it's Paris, it's Paris,
  And spring-time's come again.

Sara Teasdale (1884–1933)

The Throstle

'Summer is coming, summer is coming.
  I know it, I know it, I know it.
Light again, leaf again, life again, love again,'
  Yes, my wild little Poet.

Sing the new year in under the blue.
  Last year you sang it as gladly.
'New, new, new, new!' Is it then so new
  That you should carol so madly?

'Love again, song again, nest again, young again,'
  Never a prophet so crazy!
And hardly a daisy as yet, little friend,
  See, there is hardly a daisy.

'Here again, here, here, here, happy year'!
  O warble unchidden, unbidden!
Summer is coming, is coming, my dear,
  And all the winters are hidden.

Alfred, Lord Tennyson (1809–1892)

A Boy's Song

Where the pools are bright and deep,
Where the grey trout lies asleep,
Up the river and over the lea,
That's the way for Billy and me.

Where the blackbird sings the latest,
Where the hawthorn blooms the sweetest,
Where the nestlings chirp and flee,
That's the way for Billy and me.

Where the mowers mow the cleanest,
Where the hay lies thick and greenest,
There to track the homeward bee,
That's the way for Billy and me.

Where the hazel bank is steepest,
Where the shadow falls the deepest,
Where the clustering nuts fall free,
That's the way for Billy and me.

Why the boys should drive away
Little sweet maidens from the play,
Or love to banter and fight so well,
That's the thing I never could tell.

But this I know, I love to play
Through the meadow, among the hay;
Up the water and over the lea,
That's the way for Billy and me.

James Hogg (1770–1835)

At Shearing-Time

FROM *THE FLEECE*, BOOK I

At shearing-time, along the lively vales,
Rural festivities are often heard:
Beneath each blooming arbour all is joy
And lusty merriment: while on the grass
The mingled youth in gaudy circles sport,
We think the golden age again return'd,
And all the fabled Dryades in dance.
Leering they bound along, with laughing air,
To the shrill pipe, and deep remurm'ring cords
Of the ancient harp, or tabor's hollow sound.
    While th' old apart, upon a bank reclin'd,
Attend the tuneful carol, softly mixt
With ev'ry murmur of the sliding wave,
And ev'ry warble of the feather'd choir;
Music of paradise! which still is heard,
When the heart listens; still the views appear
Of the first happy garden, when content
To nature's flowery scenes directs the sight.

John Dyer (1699–1757)

The Passionate Shepherd to his Love

Come live with me and be my love,
And we will all the pleasures prove,
That hills and valleys, dales and fields,
And all the craggy mountains yields.

There we will sit upon the rocks,
And see the shepherds feed their flocks,
By shallow rivers to whose falls
Melodious birds sing madrigals.

And I will make thee beds of roses
With a thousand fragrant posies,
A cap of flowers, and a kirtle,
Embroidered all with leaves of myrtle;

A gown made of the finest wool
Which from our pretty lambs we pull;
Fair lined slippers for the cold,
With buckles of the purest gold;

A belt of straw and ivy-buds,
With coral clasps and amber studs:
And if these pleasures may thee move,
Come live with me and be my love.

The shepherds' swains shall dance and sing
For thy delight each May morning:
If these delights thy mind may move,
Then live with me and be my love.

Christopher Marlowe (1564–1593)

Everything Is Going to Be All Right

How should I not be glad to contemplate
the clouds clearing beyond the dormer window
and a high tide reflected on the ceiling?
There will be dying, there will be dying,
but there is no need to go into that.
The lines flow from the hand unbidden
and the hidden source is the watchful heart;
the sun rises in spite of everything
and the far cities are beautiful and bright.
I lie here in a riot of sunlight
watching the day break and the clouds flying.
Everything is going to be all right.

Derek Mahon (1941–2020)

Seeking Joy

Joy, how I sought thee!
Silver I spent and gold,
On the pleasures of this world,
　In splendid garments clad;
The wine I drank was sweet,
Rich morsels I did eat –
　Oh, but my life was sad!
Joy, how I sought thee!

Joy, I have found thee!
Far from the halls of Mirth,
Back to the soft green earth,
　Where people are not many;
I find thee, Joy, in hours
With clouds, and birds, and flowers –
　Thou dost not charge one penny.
Joy, I have found thee!

W. H. Davies (1871–1940)

Freedom

FROM *DE PROFUNDIS*

With freedom, books, flowers, and the moon, who could
not be happy?

Oscar Wilde (1854–1900)

The Starlight Night

Look at the stars! look, look up at the skies!
  O look at all the fire-folk sitting in the air!
  The bright boroughs, the circle-citadels there!
Down in dim woods the diamond delves! the elves'-eyes!
The grey lawns cold where gold, where quickgold lies!
  Wind-beat whitebeam! airy abeles set on a flare!
  Flake-doves sent floating forth at a farmyard scare!
Ah well! it is all a purchase, all is a prize.

Buy then! bid then! – What? – Prayer, patience, alms, vows.
Look, look: a May-mess, like on orchard boughs!
  Look! March-bloom, like on mealed-with-yellow sallows!
These are indeed the barn; withindoors house
The shocks. This piece-bright paling shuts the spouse
  Christ home, Christ and his mother and all his hallows.

Gerard Manley Hopkins (1844–1889)

Infant Joy

FROM *SONGS OF INNOCENCE*

'I have no name:
I am but two days old.'
What shall I call thee?
'I happy am,
Joy is my name.'
Sweet joy befall thee!

Pretty Joy!
Sweet Joy, but two days old,
Sweet Joy I call thee:
Thou dost smile,
I sing the while,
Sweet joy befall thee!

William Blake (1757–1827)

Love's Good-Morrow

Pack, clouds away! and welcome day!
With night we banish sorrow;
Sweet air, blow soft, mount larks aloft
To give my love good-morrow!
Wings from the wind to please her mind,
Notes from the lark I'll borrow;
Bird, prune thy wing, nightingale, sing,
To give my love good-morrow;
To give my love good-morrow;
Notes from them both I'll borrow.

Wake from thy nest, Robin Redbreast,
Sing birds in every furrow;
And from each hill, let music shrill
Give my fair love good-morrow!
Blackbird and thrush in every bush,
Stare, linnet, and cock-sparrow!
You pretty elves, amongst yourselves,
Sing my fair love good-morrow;
To give my love good-morrow,
Sing birds in every furrow.

Thomas Heywood (c. 1575–1641)

Kara Hissar

This morning when the dew was chill
I stood and watched the towering hill,
The tooth-topped battlements above,
The blue-winged, flutt'ring, wild rock-dove;
And the cliff looked cold in the morning.

The cliff looked cold, the cliff looked brown:
I watched the swifts come pouring down,
Their squadrons swinging out in chains
That shrilled like steel above the plains,
While their speed rejoiced in the morning.

Then suddenly the turquoise sky
Gave forth a strident, clanging cry,
And five great geese flew overhead,
Their voices sounding as they fled
Away to the North through the morning.

I saw the vulture on the crag
Rise broad and steady as a flag
Flung out above the cliff's sheer face,
And soaring gain his pride of place
As lord of the glorious morning.

Far, far above me on the rock
I saw a climbing mountain flock:
I could not see the shepherd boy,
But heard his piping voice with joy
As he sang the song of the morning.

Then in the sunshine of the day
The brown crag changed to gold and grey;
The swifts still flew in screaming strings,
And this old sanctuary of wings
Shone bright in the light of the morning.

                    AFION KARA HISSAR, 8.v.1916.

John Still (1880–1941)

Youth's the Season Made for Joys

FROM *THE BEGGAR'S OPERA*, ACT II, SCENE IV, AIR IV

Youth's the season made for joys,
   Love is then our duty:
She alone who that employs,
   Well deserves her beauty.
     Let's be gay,
     While we may,
Beauty's a flower, despised in decay.

Let us drink and sport to-day,
   Ours is not to-morrow:
Love with Youth flies swift away,
   Age is nought but sorrow.
     Dance and sing,
     Time's on the wing.
Life never knows the return of spring.

John Gay (1685–1732)

May

When MAY is in his prime, then may each heart rejoice,
When MAY bedecks each branch with green, each bird
  strains forth his voice.
The lively sap creeps up into the blooming thorn,
The flowers, which cold in prison kept, now laugh the frost
  to scorn.
All nature's imps triumph while joyful MAY doth last;
When MAY is gone, of all the year the pleasant time is past.

MAY makes the cheerful hue, MAY breeds and brings new
  blood.
MAY marcheth throughout every limb, MAY makes the
  merry mood.
MAY pricketh tender hearts, their warbling notes to tune.
Full strange it is, yet some we see do make their MAY in
  June.
Thus things are strangely wrought while joyful MAY doth
  last;
When MAY is gone, of all the year the pleasant time is past.

All you that live on earth, and have your MAY at will,
Rejoice in MAY, as I do now, and use your MAY with skill.
Use MAY while that you may, for MAY hath but his time,
When all the fruit is gone it is too late the tree to climb.
Your liking and your lust is fresh while MAY does last;
Take MAY in time, when MAY is gone the pleasant time is
  past.

Richard Edwards (1525–1566)

Low-Anchored Cloud

Low-anchored cloud,
Newfoundland air,
Fountain-head and source of rivers,
Dew-cloth, dream-drapery,
And napkin spread by fays;
Drifting meadow of the air,
Where bloom the daisied banks and violets,
And in whose fenny labyrinth
The bittern booms and heron wades;
Spirit of lakes and seas and rivers,
Bear only perfumes and the scent
Of healing herbs to just men's fields!

Henry David Thoreau (1817–1862)

Opportunity

When Mrs Gorm (Aunt Eloise)
Was stung to death by savage bees,
Her husband (Prebendary Gorm)
Put on his veil, and took the swarm.
He's publishing a book, next May
On 'How to Make Bee-keeping Pay.'

Harry Graham (1874–1936)

The Butterfly Trainers

Butterflies didn't always know
How to spread their wings and go
Gliding down the slopes of air
On their spangled wings and fair;
Never dared to leave the land
Till the elves took them in hand,
Made them bridle, bit and reins
Out of shiny corn silk skeins;
Drove them through the long blue hours,
Introducing them to Flowers.

Rachel Field (1894–1942)

Corinna's Going a Maying

VERSES 1 AND 2

Get up, get up for shame! The Blooming Morne
   Upon her wings presents the god unshorn.
   See how *Aurora* throwes her faire
   Fresh-quilted colours through the aire:
   Get up, sweet-Slug-a-bed, and see
   The Dew-bespangling Herbe and Tree.
Each Flower has wept and bow'd toward the East,
Above an houre since; yet you not drest,
   Nay! not so much as out of bed?
   When all the Birds have Mattens seyd,
   And sung their thankful Hymnes, 'tis sin,
   Nay, profanation, to keep in,
Whereas a thousand Virgins on this day
Spring, sooner than the Lark, to fetch in May.

Rise; and put on your Foliage, and be seen
To come forth, like the Spring-time, fresh and greene;
  And sweet as *Flora*. Take no care
  For Jewels for your Gowne or Haire:
  Feare not; the leaves will strew
  Gemms in abundance upon you:
Besides, the childhood of the Day has kept,
Against, you come, some *Orient Pearls* unwept:
  Come, and receive them while the light
  Hangs on the Dew-locks of the night:
  And *Titan* on the Eastern hill
  Retires himselfe, or else stands still
Till you come forth. Wash, dresse, be briefe in praying:
Few Beads are best, when once we goe a Maying.

Robert Herrick (1591–1674)

The Wind Blows Happily on Every Thing

The wind blows happily on every thing
The very weeds that shake beside the fold
Bowing they dance – do any thing but sing
And all the scene is lovely to behold
Blue mists of morning evenings of gold
How beautifull the wind will play with spring
Flowers beam with every colour light beholds
Showers oer the Landscape flye on wet pearl wings
And winds stir up unnumbered pleasant things

I love the luscious green before the bloom
The leaves and grass and even beds of moss
When leaves gin bud and spring prepares to come
The Ivys evergreen the brown green gorse
Plots of green weeds that barest roads engross
In fact I love the youth of each green thing
The grass the trees the bushes and the moss
That pleases little birds and makes them sing
I love the green before the blooms of spring.

John Clare (1793–1864)

New Friends and Old Friends

Make new friends, but keep the old;
Those are silver, these are gold.
New-made friendships, like new wine,
Age will mellow and refine.
Friendships that have stood the test –
Time and change – are surely best;
Brow may wrinkle, hair grow gray,
Friendship never knows decay.
For 'mid old friends, tried and true,
Once more we our youth renew.
But old friends, alas! may die,
New friends must their place supply.
Cherish friendship in your breast –
New is good, but old is best;
Make new friends, but keep the old;
Those are silver, these are gold.

Joseph Parry (1841–1903)

To Mrs Boteler: A description of her garden

How charming is this little spot
  Disposed with art and taste,
A thousand beauties intermixed
  Prepare the eyes a feast.

The lovely limes in ample rows
  With woodbines climbing round,
A shining gravel walk enclose
  Where not a weed is found.

The crocus, primrose, daffodil,
  And cowslip sweet I sing,
And fragrant purple violet –
  All harbingers of spring;

The musky lovely blushing pink,
  Jonquil with rich perfume,
Tulips that vie with Iris' bow,
  And balsam's annual bloom;

The immortal pea, fair 'emone,
  And beamy marigold,
And polyanthus (lovely tribe!)
  Their various blooms unfold.

The gardener's pride, ranunculus,
  Bell-flower ethereal blue,
The rose campion, and golden lupe,
  And wonder of Peru;

The amaranths, as poets sing,
  That Juno deigned to wear,
That in Hesperian gardens spring,
  Bloom fair and fragrant here.

The lily fair as new-fallen snow:
  All these the borders grace,
And myrtles, roses, jessamines
  With fragrance fill the place.

A group of dwarfish apple trees
  Appear, a fairy scene,
Laden with fruit – such Paris gave
  To Venus, beauty's queen.

Stately the rising mount appears
  With towering elms overspread,
Whose gently waving branches form
  At noon a cooling shade.

The laurel plant, the victor's crown,
    And bays by poets worn,
The particoloured phillyrea
    And May-performing thorn –

These line the walks and make the bounds
    All verdant, young, and fair:
All speak the owner's judgement good
    And praise the gardener's care.

Faint emblem of a fairer mind
    That over all presides:
For every virtue's planted there,
    And every action guides.

Mary Chandler (1687–1745)

I'll Tell You How the Sun Rose

I'll tell you how the Sun rose –
A Ribbon at a time –
The Steeples swam in Amethyst –
The news, like Squirrels, ran –
The Hills untied their Bonnets –
The Bobolinks – begun –
Then I said softly to myself –
'That must have been the Sun'!
But how he set – I know not –
There seemed a purple stile
That little Yellow boys and girls
Were climbing all the while –
Till when they reached the other side –
A Dominie in Gray –
Put gently up the evening Bars –
And led the flock away –

Emily Dickinson (1830–1886)

A Private Seat

FROM *THE CHOICE*, LINES 1–16

If heaven the grateful liberty would give
That I might choose my method how to live,
And all those hours propitious Fate should lend,
In blissful ease and satisfaction spend:
  Near some fair town I'd have a private seat,
Built uniform, not little, nor too great:
Better if on a rising ground it stood;
Fields on this side, on that a neighbouring wood;
It should within no other things contain
But what were useful, necessary, plain:
Methinks 'tis nauseous, and I'd ne'er endure
The needless pomp of gaudy furniture.
A little garden, grateful to the eye,
And a cool rivulet run murm'ring by,
On whose delicious banks a stately row
Of shady limes or sycamores should grow.

John Pomfret (1667–1702)

The Rose the Queen

FROM *DAFFODILS AND PRIMROSES*

The feildes are grene, the springe growes on a-pace.
　And nature's arte beginns to take the ayre;
Each herb her sent, each flowre doth shewe her grace.
　And beawtie braggeth of her bravest fayre.
The lambes and Rabbottes sweetely runne at base,
　The fowles do plume, and fishes fall to playe;
The muses all have chose a settinge-place
　To singe and play the sheppherdes rundeley.
Poore Choridon the onlie sillye swaine.
　That only lives and doth but onlie live;
Ys now become, to finde the heavnely vaine,
　Where happie hope dothe highest comfort give.
The little wren that never sunge a note
　Is peepinge nowe to prove how she can singe;
The nightingale hath sett in tune her throte,
　And all the woodes with little Robins ringe.
Love is abroade as naked as my nayle.
　And little byrdes doe flycker from their nestes;
Diana sweete hath sett aside her vaile,
　And Phillis shewes the beawtie of her brestes.
Oh blessèd brestes, the beawtie of the Springe!
　Oh blessèd Springe that suche a beawtie showes!
Of highest trees the hollye is the Kinge,
　And of all flowres faire fall the Queene the Rose.

Nicholas Breton (1545–1626)

Recipe for a Salad

To make this condiment your poet begs
The pounded yellow of two hard-boil'd eggs;
Two boil'd potatoes, pass'd through kitchen sieve,
Smoothness and softness to the salad give.
Let onion atoms lurk within the bowl,
And, half suspected, animate the whole.
Of mordant mustard add a single spoon,
Distrust the condiment that bites so soon;
But deem it not, thou man of herbs, a fault,
To add a double quantity of salt;
Four times the spoon with oil from Lucca brown,
And twice with vinegar, procured from town;
And lastly, o'er the flavoured compound toss
A magic soupçon of anchovy sauce.
Oh, green and glorious! Oh, herbaceous treat!
'Twould tempt the dying anchorite to eat:
Back to the world he'd turn his fleeting soul,
And plunge his fingers in the salad-bowl;
Serenely full, the epicure would say,
Fate cannot harm me, I have dined to-day.

Rev. Sydney Smith (1771–1845)

How Pleasant

FROM *DIPSYCHUS*, SCENE IV
SPIRIT, VERSES I–IV

As I sat at the café, I said to myself,
They may talk as they please about what they call pelf,
They may sneer as they like about eating and drinking,
But help it I cannot, I cannot help thinking
  How pleasant it is to have money, heigh ho!
  How pleasant it is to have money.

I sit at my table *en grand seigneur,*
And when I have done, throw a crust to the poor;
Not only the pleasure, one's self, of good living,
But also the pleasure of now and then giving.
  So pleasant it is to have money, heigh ho!
So pleasant it is to have money.

It was but last winter I came up to Town,
But already I'm getting a little renown;
I make new acquaintance where'er I appear;
I am not too shy, and have nothing to fear.
  So pleasant it is to have money, heigh ho!
  So pleasant it is to have money.

I drive through the streets, and I care not a d-mn;
The people they stare, and they ask who I am;
And if I should chance to run over a cad,
I can pay for the damage if ever so bad.
  So pleasant it is to have money, heigh ho!
  So pleasant it is to have money.

Arthur Hugh Clough (1819–1861)

The Best Thing in the World

What's the best thing in the world?
June-rose, by May-dew impearled;
Sweet south-wind, that means no rain;
Truth, not cruel to a friend;
Pleasure, not in haste to end;
Beauty, not self-decked and curled
Till its pride is over-plain;
Light, that never makes you wink;
Memory, that gives no pain;
Love, when, so, you're loved again.
What's the best thing in the world?
– Something out of it, I think.

Elizabeth Barrett Browning (1806–1861)

JUNE

The Far Horizon Fading Away

The First Day of Summer

Sweetest of all delights are the vainest, merest;
Hours when breath is joy, for the breathing's sake.
Summer awoke this morning, and early awake
I rose refreshed, and gladly my eyes saluted
The entering beam of the sun that laughed his clearest.
I too laughed for pleasure, and vowed straightway
To stream and sun the flower of an idle day,
With summer sweetly enjoyed and friends well suited.

Merry were we, as stepping aboard we laid
The shaven oars in order; merry the leap
Of the oar, that grasped the water and stirred from sleep
A wave, to tremble past us in foamy rings.
With rhyming fall, and with bright returning blade
Impetuous music urges the rippling keel;
Softly our necks the flow of the breezes feel;
And blue, and thronged with birds, the morning sings.

And lo, the elms, in a day reclothed and gleaming
In delicate youth, above us stir their leaves.
The eye, to naked winter used, receives
A magic pleasure: and still the shore we follow
Winding in flowery meadows; freshly streaming
The river meets us ever from fields unknown:
As light we travel his curving mirror lone,
No longer I envy you, O frolic swallow.

Till moored at noon by shadowy turf, and ended
Awhile that pleasant toil, what relish keen
At ease to lie amid flowers, with rustling green
O'ershaded; there, reclined by a bubbling pool,
The rushing weir in murmur and foam blended,
Entrancing ear and eye, caresses the brain
With smooth perpetual sound, the lulling strain
Of water weariless poured and glittering cool.

O then, refreshed, in the level light serene
Our boat re-entering, her prow homeward turned,
How soft we glided; soft, as evening burned
Through drooping leaves, our liquid furrow stirred
The dim green heights of the elm, reflected green
In shadowy water; at last the dreaming shore
From its own enchanted mirror we know no more:
Softly we glided downward, and spoke no word.

Nor took we land, till the West in a blush was dying,
And over the twilit meadow we loitered home.
Even now in my ear is rushing the constant foam,
And the dappled stream is alight with the wind's laughter,
As I taste, in the cool of the darkness dreamily lying,
The sun yet warm upon limbs that sweetly ache;
Drowsed deliciously, still I linger awake,
Only to keep my delight, and to look not after.

Laurence Binyon (1869–1943)

When June is Come

When June is come, then all the day
I'll sit with my love in the scented hay:
And watch the sunshot palaces high,
That the white clouds build in the breezy sky.

She singeth, and I do make her a song,
And read sweet poems the whole day long:
Unseen as we lie in our haybuilt home.
O life is delight when June is come.

Robert Bridges (1844–1930)

Upon the Water, in the Boat

Upon the water, in the boat,
I sit and sketch as down I float:
The stream is wide, the view is fair,
I sketch it looking backward there.

The stream is strong, and as I sit
And view the picture that we quit,
It flows and flows, and bears the boat,
And I sit sketching as we float.

Still as we go the things I see,
E'en as I see them, cease to be;
Their angles swerve, and with the boat
The whole perspective seems to float.

Each pointed height, each wavy line,
To wholly other forms combine;
Proportions vary, colours fade,
And all the landscape is remade.

Depicted neither far nor near
And larger there and smaller here,
And varying down from old to new,
E'en I can hardly think it true.

Yet still I look, and still I sit,
Adjusting, shaping, altering it;
And still the current bears the boat
And me, still sketching as I float.

Arthur Hugh Clough (1819–1861)

To a Skylark

Hail to thee, blithe Spirit!
  Bird thou never wert,
That from Heaven, or near it,
  Pourest thy full heart
In profuse strains of unpremeditated art.

Higher still and higher
  From the earth thou springest
Like a cloud of fire;
  The blue deep thou wingest,
And singing still dost soar, and soaring ever singest.

In the golden lightning
  Of the sunken sun,
O'er which clouds are bright'ning,
  Thou dost float and run;
Like an unbodied joy whose race is just begun.

The pale purple even
  Melts around thy flight;
Like a star of heaven
  In the broad daylight
Thou art unseen, but yet I hear thy shrill delight,

Keen as are the arrows
  Of that silver sphere,
Whose intense lamp narrows
  In the white dawn clear
Until we hardly see – we feel that it is there.

All the earth and air
  With thy voice is loud,
As, when night is bare,
  From one lonely cloud
The moon rains out her beams, and Heaven is overflowed.

What thou art we know not;
  What is most like thee?
From rainbow clouds there flow not
  Drops so bright to see
As from thy presence showers a rain of melody.

Like a Poet hidden
  In the light of thought,
Singing hymns unbidden,
  Till the world is wrought
To sympathy with hopes and fears it heeded not:

Like a high-born maiden
  In a palace-tower,
Soothing her love-laden
  Soul in secret hour
With music sweet as love, which overflows her bower:

Like a glow-worm golden
  In a dell of dew,
Scattering unbeholden
  Its aëreal hue
Among the flowers and grass, which screen it from the view!

Like a rose embowered
  In its own green leaves,
By warm winds deflowered,
  Till the scent it gives
Makes faint with too much sweet those heavy-wingèd
  thieves:

Sound of vernal showers
  On the twinkling grass,
Rain-awakened flowers,
  All that ever was
Joyous, and clear, and fresh, thy music doth surpass:

Teach us, Sprite or Bird,
  What sweet thoughts are thine:
I have never heard
  Praise of love or wine
That painted forth a flood of rapture so divine.

Chorus Hymeneal,
  Or triumphal chant,
Matched with thine would be all
  But an empty vaunt,
A thing wherein we feel there is some hidden want.

What objects are the fountains
  Of thy happy strain?
What fields, or waves, or mountains?
  What shapes of sky or plain?
What love of thine own kind? what ignorance of pain?

With thy clear keen joyance
   Languor cannot be:
Shadow of annoyance
   Never came near thee:
Thou lovest – but ne'er knew love's sad satiety.

Walking or asleep,
   Thou of death must deem
Things more true and deep
   Than we mortals dream,
Or how could thy notes flow in such a crystal stream?

We look before and after,
   And pine for what is not:
Our sincerest laughter
   With some pain is fraught;
Our sweetest songs are those that tell of saddest thought.

Yet if we could scorn
   Hate, and pride, and fear;
If we were things born
   Not to shed a tear,
I know not how thy joy we ever should come near.

Better than all measures
   Of delightful sound,
Better than all treasures
   That in books are found,
Thy skill to poet were, thou scorner of the ground!

Teach me half the gladness
  That thy brain must know,
Such harmonious madness
  From my lips would flow
The world should listen then – as I am listening now.

Percy Bysshe Shelley (1792–1822)

Sonnet XVIII

Shall I compare thee to a Summers day?
Thou art more lovely and more temperate:
Rough windes do shake the darling buds of Maie,
And Sommers lease hath all too short a date:
Sometime too hot the eye of heaven shines,
And often is his gold complexion dimm'd,
And every faire from faire some-time declines,
By chance, or natures changing course untrim'd:
But thy eternall Sommer shall not fade,
Nor lose possession of that faire thou ow'st,
Nor shall death brag thou wandr'st in his shade,
When in eternall lines to time thou grow'st,
   So long as men can breathe or eyes can see,
   So long lives this, and gives life to thee.

William Shakespeare (1564–1616)

The Windhover

TO CHRIST OUR LORD

I caught this morning morning's minion, king-
   dom of daylight's dauphin, dapple-dawn-drawn Falcon, in his riding
   Of the rolling level underneath him steady air, and striding
High there, how he rung upon the rein of a wimpling wing
In his ecstasy! then off, off forth on swing,
   As a skate's heel sweeps smooth on a bow-bend: the hurl and gliding
   Rebuffed the big wind. My heart in hiding
Stirred for a bird, – the achieve of, the mastery of the thing!

Brute beauty and valour and act, oh, air, pride, plume, here
   Buckle! AND the fire that breaks from thee then, a billion
Times told lovelier, more dangerous, O my chevalier!

   No wonder of it: shéer plód makes plough down sillion
Shine, and blue-bleak embers, ah my dear,
   Fall, gall themselves, and gash gold-vermilion.

Gerard Manley Hopkins (1844–1889)

Variations on an Air Composed on Having to Appear in a Pageant as Old King Cole

Old King Cole was a merry old soul
And a merry old soul was he;
He called for his pipe,
And he called for his bowl,
And he called for his fiddlers three.

AFTER LORD TENNYSON

Cole, that unwearied prince of Colchester,
Growing more gay with age and with long days
Deeper in laughter and desire of life,
As that Virginian climber on our walls
Flames scarlet with the fading of the year;
Called for his wassail and that other weed
Virginian also, from the western woods
Where English Raleigh checked the boast of Spain,
And lighting joy with joy, and piling up
Pleasure as crown for pleasure, bade me bring
Those three, the minstrels whose emblazoned coats
Shone with the oyster-shells of Colchester;
And these three played, and playing grew more fain
Of mirth and music; till the heathen came
And the King slept beside the northern sea.

G. K. Chesterton (1874–1936)

Variations on an Air Composed on Having to Appear in a Pageant as Old King Cole

AFTER W. B. YEATS

Of an old King in a story
　From the grey sea-folk I have heard
Whose heart was no more broken
　Than the wings of a bird.

As soon as the moon was silver
　And the thin stars began,
He took his pipe and his tankard,
　Like an old peasant man.

And three tall shadows were with him
　And came at his command;
And played before him for ever
　The fiddles of fairyland.

And he died in the young summer
　Of the world's desire;
Before our hearts were broken
　Like sticks in a fire.

G. K. Chesterton (1874–1936)

Variations on an Air Composed on Having to Appear in a Pageant as Old King Cole

AFTER ROBERT BROWNING

Who smoke-snorts toasts o' My Lady Nicotine,
Kicks stuffing out of Pussyfoot, bids his trio
Stick up their Stradivarii (that's the plural
Or near enough, my fatheads; *nimium*
Vicina Cremonœ; that's a bit too near.)
Is there some stockfish fails to understand?
Catch hold o' the notion, bellow and blurt back 'Cole'?
Must I bawl lessons from a horn-book, howl,
Cat-call the cat-gut 'fiddles'? Fiddlesticks!

G. K. Chesterton (1874–1936)

Variations on an Air Composed on Having to Appear in a Pageant as Old King Cole

AFTER WALT WHITMAN

Me clairvoyant,
Me conscious of you, old camarado,
Needing no telescope, lorgnette, field-glass, opera-glass,
    myopic pince-nez,
Me piercing two thousand years with eye naked and not
    ashamed;
The crown cannot hide you from me,
Musty old feudal-heraldic trappings cannot hide you
    from me,
I perceive that you drink.
(I am drinking with you. I am as drunk as you are.)
I see you are inhaling tobacco, puffing, smoking, spitting
(I do not object to your spitting),
You prophetic of American largeness,
You anticipating the broad masculine manners of these
    States;
I see in you also there are movements, tremors, tears,
    desire for the melodious,
I salute your three violinists, endlessly making vibrations,
Rigid, relentless, capable of going on for ever;
They play my accompaniment; but I shall take no notice
    of any accompaniment;
I myself am a complete orchestra.
So long.

G. K. Chesterton (1874–1936)

Variations on an Air Composed on Having to Appear in a Pageant as Old King Cole

AFTER SWINBURNE

In the time of old sin without sadness
And golden with wastage of gold
Like the gods that grow old in their gladness
Was the king that was glad, growing old;
And with sound of loud lyres from his palace
The voice of his oracles spoke,
And the lips that were red from his chalice
Were splendid with smoke.

When the weed was as flame for a token
And the wine was as blood for a sign;
And upheld in his hands and unbroken
The fountains of fire and of wine.
And a song without speech, without singer,
Stung the soul of a thousand in three
As the flesh of the earth has to sting her,
The soul of the sea.

G. K. Chesterton (1874–1936)

June

In June I give you a close-wooded fell,
  With crowns of thicket coiled about its head,
  With thirty villas twelve times turreted,
All girdling round a little citadel;
And in the midst a springhead and fair well
  With thousand conduits branched and shining speed,
  Wounding the garden and the tender mead,
Yet to the freshened grass acceptable.
And lemons, citrons, dates, and oranges,
  And all the fruits whose savour is most rare,
Shall shine within the shadow of your trees;
  And every one shall be a lover there;
Until your life, so filled with courtesies,
  Throughout the world be counted debonair.

Folgóre da San Gimignano (c. 1270–c. 1332)
Translated by Dante Gabriel Rossetti (1828–1882)

June 1966

Lying flat in the bracken of Richmond Park
while the legs and voices of my children pass
seeking, seeking: I remember how on the
13th of June of that simmering 1940
I was conscripted into the East Surreys,
and, more than a quarter of a century
ago, when France had fallen,
we practised concealment in this very bracken.
The burnt stalks pricked through my denims.
Hitler is now one of the antiques of History,
I lurk like a monster in my hiding place.
He didn't get me. If there were a God
it would be only polite to thank him.

Gavin Ewart (1916-1995)

In the Grass

Face downward on the grass in reverie,
    I found how cool and sweet
Are the green glooms that often thoughtlessly
    I tread beneath my feet.

In this strange mimic wood where grasses lean –
    Elf trees untouched of bark –
I heard the hum of insects, saw the sheen
    Of sunlight framing dark,

And felt with thoughts I cannot understand,
    And know not how to speak,
A daisy reaching up its little hand
    To lay it on my cheek.

Ethelwyn Wetherald (1857–1940)

A Day That is Boundless as Youth

A day that is boundless as youth
And gay with delight to be born,
Where the waves flash and glide over sands
In their pure image rippled and worn;
Where laughter is young on the air
As the race of young feet patters light!
Linked shadows run dancing before
In the midst of the infinite light!
On a violet horizon asleep
One milky sail glimmers afar;
And our spirits are free of the world
With nothing to bind or to bar;
With no thought but the thoughts of a child;
O golden the day and the hour!
The strong sea is charmed from his rage,
And the waste is more fair than a flower.

Laurence Binyon (1869–1943)

Roses on the Breakfast Table

Just a few of the roses we gathered from the Isar
Are fallen, and their mauve-red petals on the cloth
Float like boats on a river, while other
Roses are ready to fall, reluctant and loth.

She laughs at me across the table, saying
I am beautiful. I look at the rumpled young roses
And suddenly realise, in them as in me,
How lovely is the self this day discloses.

D. H. Lawrence (1885–1930)

Where Innocent Bright-eyed Daisies Are

Where innocent bright-eyed daisies are,
  With blades of grass between,
Each daisy stands up like a star
  Out of a sky of green.

Christina Rossetti (1830–1894)

Song

O Lady, leave thy silken thread
And flowery tapestrie,
There's living roses on the bush,
And blossoms on the tree;
Stoop where thou wilt, thy careless hand
Some random bud will meet;
Thou canst not tread, but thou wilt find
The daisy at thy feet.

'Tis like the birthday of the world,
When earth was born in bloom;
The light is made of many dyes,
The air is all perfume;
There's crimson buds, and white and blue –
The very rainbow show'rs
Have turn'd to blossoms where they fell,
And sown the earth with flow'rs.

There's fairy tulips in the East,
The garden of the sun;
The very streams reflect the hues,
And blossom as they run:
While morn opes like a crimson rose,
Still wet with pearly showers;
Then, lady, leave the silken thread
Thou twinest into flow'rs!

Thomas Hood (1799–1845)

Song

The summer down the garden walks
  Swept in her garments bright;
She touched the pale still lily stalks
  And crowned them with delight;
She breathed upon the rose's head
  And filled its heart with fire,
And with a golden carpet spread
  The path of my desire.

The larkspurs stood like sentinels
  To greet her as she came,
Soft rang the Canterbury bells
  The music of her name.
She passed across the happy land
  Where all dear dreams flower free;
She took my true love by the hand
And led her out to me.

E. Nesbit (1858–1924)

A Summer Morning

I saw dawn creep across the sky,
And all the gulls go flying by.
I saw the sea put on its dress
Of blue mid-summer loveliness,
And heard the trees begin to stir
Green arms of pine and juniper.
I heard the wind call out and say:
'Get up, my dear, it is to-day.'

Rachel Field (1894–1942)

Moonrise

I awoke in the Midsummer not to call night, | in the
   white and the walk of the morning:
The moon, dwindled and thinned to the fringe | of a
   finger-nail held to the candle,
Or paring of paradisaïcal fruit, | lovely in waning but
   lustreless,
Stepped from the stool, drew back from the barrow, | of
   dark Maenefa the mountain;
A cusp still clasped him, a fluke yet fanged him, |
   entangled him, not quit utterly.
This was the prized, the desirable sight, | unsought,
   presented so easily,
Parted me leaf and leaf, divided me, | eyelid and eyelid of
   slumber.

Gerard Manley Hopkins (1844–1889)

The Green Tent

Summer has spread a cool, green tent
　Upon the bare poles of this tree;
Where 'tis a joy to sit all day,
　And hear the small birds' melody;
To see the sheep stand bolt upright,
　Nibbling at grass almost their height.

And much I marvel now how men
　Can waste their fleeting days in greed;
That one man should desire more gold
　Than twenty men should truly need;
For is not this green tent more sweet
　Than any chamber of the great?

This tent, at which I spend my day,
　Was made at Nature's cost, not mine;
And when night comes, and I must sleep,
　No matter if my room be fine
Or common, for Content and Health
　Can sleep without the power of Wealth.

W. H. Davies (1871–1940)

Under the Willows

LINES 1–20

Frank-hearted hostess of the field and wood,
Gypsy, whose roof is every spreading tree,
June is the pearl of our New England year.
Still a surprisal, though expected long.
Her coming startles. Long she lies in wait,
Makes many a feint, peeps forth, draws coyly back,
Then, from some southern ambush in the sky,
With one great gush of blossom storms the world.
A week ago the sparrow was divine;
The bluebird, shifting his light load of song
From post to post along the cheerless fence,
Was as a rhymer ere the poet come;
But now, O rapture! sunshine winged and voiced,
Pipe blown through by the warm wild breath of the West
Shepherding his soft droves of fleecy cloud,
Gladness of woods, skies, waters, all in one,
The bobolink has come, and, like the soul
Of the sweet season vocal in a bird,
Gurgles in ecstasy we know not what
Save June! Dear June! Now God be praised for June.

James Russell Lowell (1819–1891)

A Flaw

FROM *EPISTLE TO J. H. REYNOLDS*

It is a flaw
In happiness, to see beyond our bourn, –
It forces us in summer skies to mourn,
It spoils the singing of the Nightingale.

John Keats (1795–1821)

Receipt for a Cake

VERSES 1–4

Take Flour made from Wheat most fine
Take Currants fresh from Zante's Isle
Take Butter from the choicest Kine
Take Almonds from the Trees that Smile

On Jordan's banks: – take of the Spice
That in the Indian Isles abound;
Take new-laid Eggs, quite fresh and nice,
Take Sweetmeats, richest that are found;

Take of the Wine that Falstaff loved –
Take eau de vie from Gallia's shore,
Take of the Sugar most approved
That's grown upon Jamaica's shore,

And when you've beat and mixed them well,
And let them in your Oven bake:
Rest them awhile, before you tell
The glories of the splendid Cake.

Sara Coleridge (1802–1852)

To the Grasshopper and the Cricket

Green little vaulter in the sunny grass,
  Catching your heart up at the feel of June,
  Sole voice that's heard amidst the lazy noon,
When ev'n the bees lag at the summoning brass; –
And you, warm little housekeeper, who class
  With those who think the candles come too soon,
  Loving the fire, and with your tricksome tune
Nick the glad silent moments as they pass; –

Oh, sweet and tiny cousins, that belong
  One to the fields, the other to the hearth,
Both have your sunshine; both, though small, are strong
  At your clear hearts, and both were sent on earth
To sing in thoughtful ears this natural song –
  Indoors and out – summer and winter, – Mirth.

Leigh Hunt (1784–1859)

Seaside Golf

How straight it flew, how long it flew,
  It clear'd the rutty track
And soaring, disappeared from view
  Beyond the bunker's back –
A glorious, sailing, bounding drive
  That made me glad I was alive.

And down the fairway, far along
  It glowed a lonely white;
I played an iron sure and strong
  And clipp'd it out of sight,
And spite of grassy banks between
I knew I'd find it on the green.

And so I did. It lay content
  Two paces from the pin;
A steady putt and then it went
  Oh, most securely in.
The very turf rejoiced to see
That quite unprecedented three.

Ah! Seaweed smells from sandy caves
  And thyme and mist in whiffs,
In-coming tide, Atlantic waves
  Slapping the sunny cliffs,
Lark song and sea sounds in the air
And splendour, splendour everywhere.

John Betjeman (1906–1984)

A Farm Picture

Through the ample open door of the peaceful country barn,
A sunlit pasture field with cattle and horses feeding,
And haze and vista, and the far horizon fading away.

Walt Whitman (1819–1892)

Adlestrop

Yes. I remember Adlestrop –
The name, because one afternoon
Of heat the express-train drew up there
Unwontedly. It was late June.

The steam hissed. Someone cleared his throat.
No one left and no one came
On the bare platform. What I saw
Was Adlestrop – only the name

And willows, willow-herb, and grass,
And meadowsweet, and haycocks dry,
No whit less still and lonely fair
Than the high cloudlets in the sky.

And for that minute a blackbird sang
Close by, and round him, mistier,
Farther and farther, all the birds
Of Oxfordshire and Gloucestershire.

Edward Thomas (1878–1917)

A Water-Party

Let us, as by this verdant bank we float,
Search down the marge to find some shady pool
Where we may rest awhile and moor our boat,
And bathe our tired limbs in the waters cool.
  Beneath the noonday sun,
  Swiftly, O river, run!
Here is a mirror for Narcissus, see!
I cannot sound it, plumbing with my oar.
Lay the stern in beneath this bowering tree!
Now, stepping on this stump, we are ashore.
  Guard, Hamadryades,
  Our clothes laid by your trees!
How the birds warble in the woods! I pick
The waxen lilies, diving to the root.
But swim not far in the stream, the weeds grow thick,
And hot on the bare head the sunbeams shoot.
  Until our sport be done,
  O merry birds, sing on!
If but to-night the sky be clear, the moon
Will serve us well, for she is near the full.
We shall row safely home; only too soon, –
So pleasant 'tis, whether we float or pull.
  To guide us through the night,
  O summer moon, shine bright!

Robert Bridges (1844–1930)

JULY

Pleasant Be Thy Dreams

The Secret Joy

Face to face with the sunflower,
Cheek to cheek with the rose,
We follow a secret highway
Hardly a traveller knows.
The gold that lies in the folded bloom
Is all our wealth;
We eat of the heart of the forest
With innocent stealth.
We know the ancient roads
In the leaf of a nettle,
And bathe in the blue profound
Of a speedwell petal.

Mary Webb (1881–1927)

'O! once again good night!'

O! once again good night!
And be thy slumbers light,
Pleasant thy dreams and bright
　As sun-clad mist: –
And when they disappear,
O! may thy mind be clear
From every doubt and fear,
　As lake by breezes kist!

Sara Coleridge (1802–1852)

The Piper

I had a willow whistle,
   I piped it on the hill
The grass reached up, the sky bent down,
   And all the world grew still.

Now up, now down the rounded holes,
   My fingers fluttered light,
And little notes came trooping out
   As thick as elves by night.

They turned themselves into a tune
   More clear than drops of dew,
More sweet than almond trees, more soft
   Than clouds the moon slips through.

Oh, good it was to be alone –
   To pipe there on the hill,
With bending sky, and reaching grass,
   And all the world grown still.

Rachel Field (1894–1942)

The Declaration of Independence

CONGRESS, JULY 4, 1776

The unanimous Declaration of the thirteen united States of America, When in the Course of human events, it becomes necessary for one people to dissolve the political bands which have connected them with another, and to assume among the powers of the earth, the separate and equal station to which the Laws of Nature and of Nature's God entitle them, a decent respect to the opinions of mankind requires that they should declare the causes which impel them to the separation.

We hold these truths to be self-evident, that all men are created equal, that they are endowed by their Creator with certain unalienable Rights, that among these are Life, Liberty and the pursuit of Happiness.

Choric Song

FROM *THE LOTUS-EATERS*

I.

There is sweet music here that softer falls
Than petals from blown roses on the grass,
Or night-dews on still waters between walls
Of shadowy granite, in a gleaming pass;
Music that gentlier on the spirit lies,
Than tir'd eyelids upon tired eyes;
Music that brings sweet sleep down from the blissful skies.
Here are cool mosses deep,
And thro' the moss the ivies creep,
And in the stream the long-leaved flowers weep,
And from the craggy ledge the poppy hangs in sleep.

Alfred, Lord Tennyson (1809–1892)

Under a Flowering Tree

Under a flowering Tree
I sat with my dearest Love.
Night flowered in stars above
And the heart was a-flower in me.

Laurence Binyon (1869–1943)

Margarita

The recipe for a good margarita
Is no secret;
But it is an art
To achieve it

The base note:
The exquisite essence
Of agave
From that exotic succulent
Of Mexico:
A shot of Tequila *reposado*,
Turned by alchemy of oak,
To liquid gold.

Next:
A half measure of triple-sec
For the aroma of oranges,
Sun-soaked;

And finally:
The fresh-pressed
Juice of limes – a little less;
The citrus top note.

[Shake well with ice,
And serve on the rocks
With slice of lime]

So here you have
The Margarita:

A cocktail born
Of scorching heat;
Its liquor,
Cradled in oak barrels,
Which leave their legacy
Of earthy peat;

Picture,
Pitted orange-peels
Hung to dry
In Seville's bright sun;
And the glistening
Fruits of lime-trees
Ripening,
In lands far-flung;

Savour,
Through the salted rim,
The prickly plant's
Divine bouquet;
Allow to linger
On the taste-buds
The memory of bitter spines
And nectar, sweet;

Now drink, at last,
From the frosted glass,
This incomparable aperitif,
Spirits lifted
By the zest of lime,
In this sublime
Restorative.

Jana Synková (1968–)

Ducks' Ditty

FROM *WIND IN THE WILLOWS*

All along the backwater,
Through the rushes tall,
Ducks are a-dabbling.
Up tails all!

Ducks' tails, drakes' tails,
Yellow feet a-quiver,
Yellow bills out of sight
Busy in the river!

Slushy green undergrowth
Where the roach swim –
Here we keep our larder,
Cool and full and dim.

Everyone for what he likes!
We like to be
Head down, tails up,
Dabbling free!

High in the blue above
Swifts whirl and call –
We are down a-dabbling
Up tails all!

Kenneth Grahame (1859–1932)

Awakening Morning Laughs from Heaven

Awaking morning laughs from heaven
On golden summer's forests green
And what a gush of song is given
To welcome in that light serene

A fresh wind waves the clustering roses
And through the open window sighs
Around the couch where she reposes
The lady with the dovelike eyes

With dovelike eyes and shining hair
And velvet cheek so sweetly moulded
And hands so soft and white and fair
Above her snowy bosom folded
* * * *
Her sister's and her brother's feet
Are brushing off the scented dew
And she springs up in haste to greet
Grass and flowers and sunshine too

Emily Brontë (1818–1848)

Recuerdo

We were very tired, we were very merry –
We had gone back and forth all night on the ferry.
It was bare and bright, and smelled like a stable –
But we looked into a fire, we leaned across a table,
We lay on a hill-top underneath the moon;
And the whistles kept blowing, and the dawn came soon.

We were very tired, we were very merry –
We had gone back and forth all night on the ferry;
And you ate an apple, and I ate a pear,
From a dozen of each we had bought somewhere;
And the sky went wan, and the wind came cold,
And the sun rose dripping, a bucketful of gold.

We were very tired, we were very merry,
We had gone back and forth all night on the ferry.
We hailed, 'Good morrow, mother!' to a shawl-covered head,
And bought a morning paper, which neither of us read;
And she wept, 'God bless you!' for the apples and pears,
And we gave her all our money but our subway fares.

Edna St Vincent Millay (1892–1950)

Oh, Sweet Content

Oh, sweet content, that turns the labourer's sweat
  To tears of joy, and shines the roughest face;
How often have I sought you high and low,
  And found you still in some lone quiet place.

Here, in my room, when full of happy dreams,
  With no life heard beyond that merry sound
Of moths that on my lighted ceiling kiss
  Their shadows as they dance and dance around.

Or in a garden, on a summer's night,
  When I have seen the dark and solemn air
Blink with the blind bat's wings, and heaven's bright face
  Twitch with the stars that shine in thousands there.

W. H. Davies (1871–1940)

July

For July, in Siena, by the willow-tree,
   I give you barrels of white Tuscan wine
   In ice far down your cellars stored supine;
And morn and eve to eat in company
Of those vast jellies dear to you and me
   Of partridges and youngling pheasants sweet,
   Boiled capons, sovereign kids: and let their treat
Be veal and garlic, with whom these agree.
Let time slip by, till by-and-by, all day;
   And never swelter through the heat at all,
But move at ease at home, sound, cool, and gay;
   And wear sweet-coloured robes that lightly fall;
And keep your tables set in fresh array,
   Not coaxing spleen to be your seneschal.

Folgóre da San Gimignano (c. 1270–c. 1332)
Translated by Dante Gabriel Rossetti (1828–1882)

Between the Dusk of a Summer Night

PRAELUDIUM, XXII

Between the dusk of a summer night
  And the dawn of a summer day,
We caught at a mood as it passed in flight,
  And we bade it stoop and stay.
And what with the dawn of night began
  With the dusk of day was done;
For that is the way of woman and man,
  When a hazard has made them one.

Arc upon arc, from shade to shine,
  The World went thundering free;
And what was his errand but hers and mine –
  The lords of him, I and she?
O, it's die we must, but it's live we can,
  And the marvel of earth and sun
Is all for the joy of woman and man
  And the longing that makes them one.

W. E. Henley (1849–1903)

Winged Words

As darting swallows skim across a pool,
   Whose tranquil depths reflect a tranquil sky,
So, o'er the depths of silence, dark and cool,
    Our winged words dart playfully,
     And seldom break
   The quiet surface of the lake,
  As they flit by.

Mary Coleridge (1861–1907)

Haze

Woof of the sun, ethereal gauze,
Woven of Nature's richest stuffs,
Visible heat, air-water, and dry sea,
Last conquest of the eye;
Toil of the day displayed, sun-dust,
Aerial surf upon the shores of earth,
Ethereal estuary, frith of light,
Breakers of air, billows of heat,
Fine summer spray on inland seas;
Bird of the sun, transparent-winged
Owlet of noon, soft-pinioned,
From hearth or stubble rising without song;
Establish thy serenity o'er the fields.

Henry David Thoreau (1817–1862)

Miracles

Why, who makes much of a miracle?
As to me I know of nothing else but miracles,
Whether I walk the streets of Manhattan,
Or dart my sight over the roofs of houses toward the sky,
Or wade with naked feet along the beach just in the edge
    of the water,
Or stand under trees in the woods,
Or talk by day with any one I love, or sleep in the bed at
    night with any one I love,
Or sit at table at dinner with the rest,
Or look at strangers opposite me riding in the car,
Or watch honey-bees busy around the hive of a summer
    forenoon,
Or animals feeding in the fields,
Or birds, or the wonderfulness of insects in the air,
Or the wonderfulness of the sundown, or of stars shining
    so quiet and bright,
Or the exquisite delicate thin curve of the new moon in
    spring;
These with the rest, one and all, are to me miracles,
The whole referring, yet each distinct and in its place.

To me every hour of the light and dark is a miracle,
Every cubic inch of space is a miracle,
Every square yard of the surface of the earth is spread
    with the same,
Every foot of the interior swarms with the same.

To me the sea is a continual miracle,
The fishes that swim – the rocks – the motion of the
    waves – the ships with men in them,
What stranger miracles are there?

Walt Whitman (1819–1892)

A Bird's Flight

From some bright cloudlet dropping;
From branch to blossom hopping;
Then drinking from a small brown stone
    That stood alone
Amid the brook; then, singing,
    Upspringing,
It soared: my bird had flown.

A glimpse of beauty only
That left the glen more lonely?
Nay, truly; for its song and flight
    Made earth more bright!
If men were less regretful
    And fretful,
Would life yield less delight?

William Canton (1845–1926)

Song for a Blue Roadster

Fly, Roadster, fly!
  The sun is high,
Gold are the fields
  We hurry by,
Green are the woods
  As we slide through
Past harbor and headland,
  Blue on blue.

Fly, Roadster, fly!
  The hay smells sweet,
And the flowers are fringing
  Each village street,
Where carts are blue
  And barns are red,
And the road unwinds
  Like a twist of thread.

Fly, Roadster, fly!
  Leave Time behind;
Out of sight
  Shall be out of mind.
Shine and shadow
  Blue sea, green bough,
Nothing is real
  But Here and Now.

Rachel Field (1894–1942)

Summer Vacation

FROM *THE PRELUDE*, 1850, BOOK FOURTH

Bright was the summer's noon when quickening steps
Followed each other till a dreary moor
Was crossed, a bare ridge clomb, upon whose top
Standing alone, as from a rampart's edge,
I overlooked the bed of Windermere,
Like a vast river, stretching in the sun.
With exultation, at my feet I saw
Lake, islands, promontories, gleaming bays,
A universe of Nature's fairest forms
Proudly revealed with instantaneous burst,
Magnificent, and beautiful, and gay.

William Wordsworth (1770–1850)

My Delight and Thy Delight

My delight and thy delight
Walking, like two angels white,
In the gardens of the night:

My desire and thy desire
Twining to a tongue of fire,
Leaping live, and laughing higher;
Thro' the everlasting strife
In the mystery of life.

Love, from whom the world begun,
Hath the secret of the sun.

Love can tell, and love alone,
Whence the million stars were strewn,
Why each atom knows its own,
How, in spite of woe and death,
Gay is life, and sweet is breath:

This he taught us, this we knew,
Happy in his science true,
Hand in hand as we stood
'Neath the shadows of the wood
Heart to heart as we lay
In the dawning of the day.

Robert Bridges (1844–1930)

Inscription for the Entrance to a Wood

Stranger, if thou hast learned a truth which needs
No school of long experience, that the world
Is full of guilt and misery, and hast seen
Enough of all its sorrows, crimes, and cares,
To tire thee of it, enter this wild wood
And view the haunts of Nature. The calm shade
Shall bring a kindred calm, and the sweet breeze
That makes the green leaves dance, shall waft a balm
To thy sick heart. Thou wilt find nothing here
Of all that pained thee in the haunts of men
And made thee loathe thy life. The primal curse
Fell, it is true, upon the unsinning earth,
But not in vengeance. God hath yoked to Guilt
Her pale tormentor, Misery. Hence, these shades
Are still the abodes of gladness; the thick roof
Of green and stirring branches is alive
And musical with birds, that sing and sport
In wantonness of spirit; while below
The squirrel, with raised paws and form erect,
Chirps merrily. Throngs of insects in the shade
Try their thin wings and dance in the warm beam
That waked them into life. Even the green trees
Partake the deep contentment; as they bend
To the soft winds, the sun from the blue sky
Looks in and sheds a blessing on the scene.
Scarce less the cleft-born wild-flower seems to enjoy
Existence, than the winged plunderer

That sucks its sweets. The massy rocks themselves,
And the old and ponderous trunks of prostrate trees
That lead from knoll to knoll a causey rude
Or bridge the sunken brook, and their dark roots,
With all their earth upon them, twisting high,
Breathe fixed tranquillity. The rivulet
Sends forth glad sounds, and tripping o'er its bed
Of pebbly sands, or leaping down the rocks,
Seems, with continuous laughter, to rejoice
In its own being. Softly tread the marge,
Lest from her midway perch thou scare the wren
That dips her bill in water. The cool wind,
That stirs the stream in play, shall come to thee,
Like one that loves thee nor will let thee pass
Ungreeted, and shall give its light embrace.

Sir William Cullen Bryant (1794–1878)

Emblems: after her illness

They went away, the sad times.
It wasn't I who turned them out of doors,
but another.

The swifts have returned. They've dropped
their burden of long journeys. With what joy
they scream over the rooftops.

Pour the coffee. Sit by the fire
that says *home*. Tomorrow we'll welcome
all the tomorrows there are to be.

Do you hear the swifts? They tie together
the bright light. They nest
in secret places.

Norman MacCaig (1910–1996)

The Morning-Watch

LINES 1–22

O joys! Infinite sweetness! with what flowres
And shoots of glory, my soul breakes and buds!
       All the long houres
       Of night, and Rest,
      Through the still shrouds
       Of sleep, and Clouds,
    This Dew fell on my Breast;
       O how it *Blouds,*
And Spirits all my Earth! heark! In what Rings
And *Hymning Circulations* the quick world
       Awakes, and sings;
       The rising winds
      And falling springs,
      Birds, beasts, all things
    Adore him in their kinds.
      Thus all is hurl'd
In sacred *Hymnes* and *Order,* The great *Chime*
And *Symphony* of nature. Prayer is
      The world in tune,
       A spirit-voyce,
      And vocall joyes
    Whose *Eccho* is heav'ns blisse.

Henry Vaughan (1621–1695)

Joy

I am wild, I will sing to the trees,
  I will sing to the stars in the sky,
I love, I am loved, he is mine,
  Now at last I can die!

I am sandaled with wind and with flame,
  I have heart-fire and singing to give,
I can tread on the grass or the stars,
  Now at last I can live!

Sara Teasdale (1884–1933)

No Bed

No bed! no bed! we shouted,
And wheeled our eyes from home
To where the green and golden woods
   Cried, Come!

Wild sang the evening birds.
The sun-clouds shone in our eyes,
A silver snippet of moon hung low
   In the skies.

We ran, we leapt, we sang.
We yodelled loud and shrill,
Chased Nobody through the valley and
   Up the hill.

We laughed, we quarrelled, we drank
The cool sweet of the dew.
Beading on bud and leaf the dim
   Woods through.

We stayed, we listened, we looked –
Now dark was on the prowl!
Too-whit-a-woo, from its hollow called
   An owl.

O Sleep, at last to slide
Into eyes made drunk with light;
Call in thy footsore boys to harmless
   Night!

Walter de la Mare (1873–1956)

Hector in the Garden

VERSES I–V

I

Nine years old! The first of any
  Seem the happiest years that come:
  Yet when *I* was nine, I said
  No such word! – I thought instead
That the Greeks had used as many
  In besieging Ilium.

II

Nine green years had scarcely brought me
  To my childhood's haunted spring;
  I had life, like flowers and bees.
  In betwixt the country trees,
And the sun the pleasure taught me
  Which he teacheth every thing.

III

If the rain fell, there was sorrow:
  Little head leant on the pane,
  Little finger drawing down it
  The long trailing drops upon it,
And the 'Rain, rain, come to-morrow,'
  Said for charm against the rain.

IV

Such a charm was right Canidian,
  Though you meet it with a jeer!
  If I said it long enough,
  Then the rain hummed dimly off,
And the thrush with his pure Lydian
Was left only to the ear;

V

And the sun and I together
  Went a-rushing out of doors:
  We our tender spirits drew
  Over hill and dale in view,
Glimmering hither, glimmering thither
  In the footsteps of the showers.

Elizabeth Barrett Browning (1806–1861)

Drawing Near the Light

Lo, when we wade the tangled wood,
In haste and hurry to be there,
Nought seem its leaves and blossoms good,
For all that they be fashioned fair.

But looking up, at last we see
The glimmer of the open light,
From o'er the place where we would be:
Then grow the very brambles bright.

So now, amidst our day of strife,
With many a matter glad we play,
When once we see the light of life
Gleam through the tangle of to-day.

William Morris (1834–1896)

Summer Beach

For how long known this boundless wash of light,
  This smell of purity, this gleaming waste,
This wind? This brown, strewn wrack how old a sight,
  These pebbles round to touch and salt to taste.

See, the slow marbled heave, the liquid arch,
  Before the waves' procession to the land
Flowers in foam; the ripples' onward march,
  Their last caresses on the pure hard sand.

For how long known these bleaching corks, new-made
  Smooth and enchanted from the lapping sea?
Since I first laboured with a wooden spade
  Against this background of Eternity.

Frances Cornford (1886–1960)

A Summer Sleeping-Room

Here is my summer sleeping-room
  Within a grove of towering pine;
These latticed walls, this fragrant gloom,
  This ever-open door, are mine.

However hot the heart of day,
  When all its insect cares have flown,
Unto the green I nightly stray
  In moonlight silence all alone.

Four pines are close. They pierce the roof,
  One at each corner of my nest,
And all my dreams are trouble-proof
  As though four angels watched my rest.

Tree-toads and crickets sing to me,
  The screech-owl sends his note from far;
The night wind moves, and dazzlingly
  Comes to my couch the eastern star.

At dawn I hear the squirrels run,
  A larger wind its coolness pour,
And with the first red ray of sun
  Behold the Redbreast at the door.

Oh, sweet to waken with the flowers,
  A morning spirit steeped in calm,
And bear through all the dusty hours
  The night-pure heart, the breath of balm.

Ethelwyn Wetherald (1857–1940)

Ariel's Song

FROM *THE TEMPEST*, ACT V, SCENE I

Where the bee sucks, there suck I:
In a cowslip's bell I lie;
There I couch when owls do cry.
On the bat's back I do fly
After summer merrily.
Merrily, merrily shall I live now
Under the blossom that hangs on the bow.

William Shakespeare (1564–1616)

I Taste a Liquor Never Brewed

I taste a liquor never brewed –
From Tankards scooped in Pearl –
Not all the Frankfort Berries
Yield such an Alcohol!

Inebriate of Air – am I –
And Debauchee of Dew –
Reeling – thro' endless summer days –
From inns of Molten Blue –

When 'Landlords' turn the drunken Bee
Out of the Foxglove's door –
When Butterflies – renounce their 'drams' –
I shall but drink the more!

Till Seraphs swing their snowy Hats –
And Saints – to windows run –
To see the little Tippler
Leaning against the – Sun!

Emily Dickinson (1830–1886)

AUGUST

Feel the Sunshine

Day-Dreams

Broad August burns in milky skies,
    The world is blanched with hazy heat;
The vast green pasture, even, lies
    Too hot and bright for eyes and feet.

Amid the grassy levels rears
    The sycamore against the sun
The dark boughs of a hundred years,
    The emerald foliage of one.

Lulled in a dream of shade and sheen,
    Within the clement twilight thrown
By that great cloud of floating green,
    A horse is standing, still as stone.

He stirs nor head nor hoof, although
    The grass is fresh beneath the branch;
His tail alone swings to and fro
    In graceful curves from haunch to haunch.

He stands quite lost, indifferent
    To rack or pasture, trace or rein;
He feels the vaguely sweet content
    Of perfect sloth in limb and brain.

William Canton (1845–1926)

Songs of Travel

VERSE X

I know not how it is with you –
  I love the first and last,
The whole field of the present view,
  The whole flow of the past.

One tittle of the things that are,
  Nor you should change nor I –
One pebble in our path – one star
  In all our heaven of sky.

Our lives, and every day and hour,
  One symphony appear:
One road, one garden – every flower
  And every bramble dear.

Robert Louis Stevenson (1850–1894)

The River-God's Song

FROM *THE FAITHFUL SHEPHERDESS*

Do not fear to put thy feet
Naked in the river sweet;
Think not leech or newt or toad
Will bite thy foot when thou hast trod;
Nor let the water rising high,
As thou wad'st in make thee cry
And sob, but ever live with me,
And not a wave shall trouble thee.

John Fletcher (1579–1625)

Life

Life, believe, is not a dream
  So dark as sages say;
Oft a little morning rain
  Foretells a pleasant day.
Sometimes there are clouds of gloom,
  But these are transient all;
If the shower will make the roses bloom,
  O why lament its fall?
    Rapidly, merrily,
  Life's sunny hours flit by,
    Gratefully, cheerily
  Enjoy them as they fly!

What though Death at times steps in,
  And calls our Best away?
What though sorrow seems to win,
  O'er hope, a heavy sway?
Yet Hope again elastic springs,
  Unconquered, though she fell;
Still buoyant are her golden wings,
  Still strong to bear us well.
    Manfully, fearlessly,
  The day of trial bear,
    For gloriously, victoriously,
  Can courage quell despair!

Charlotte Brontë (1816–1855)

The Rolling English Road

Before the Roman came to Rye or out to Severn strode,
The rolling English drunkard made the rolling English
road.
A reeling road, a rolling road, that rambles round the
shire,
And after him the parson ran, the sexton and the squire;
A merry road, a mazy road, and such as we did tread
The night we went to Birmingham by way of Beachy
Head.

I knew no harm of Bonaparte and plenty of the Squire,
And for to fight the Frenchman I did not much desire;
But I did bash their baggonets because they came
arrayed
To straighten out the crooked road an English drunkard
made,
Where you and I went down the lane with ale-mugs in
our hands,
The night we went to Glastonbury by way of Goodwin
Sands.

His sins they were forgiven him; or why do flowers run
Behind him; and the hedges all strengthening in the sun?
The wild thing went from left to right and knew not
which was which,
But the wild rose was above him when they found him in
the ditch.
God pardon us, nor harden us; we did not see so clear
The night we went to Bannockburn by way of
Brighton Pier.

My friends, we will not go again or ape an ancient rage,

Or stretch the folly of our youth to be the shame of age,

But walk with clearer eyes and ears this path that
wandereth,

And see undrugged in evening light the decent inn
of death;

For there is good news yet to hear and fine things
to be seen,

Before we go to Paradise by way of Kensal Green.

G. K. Chesterton (1874–1936)

Arrival

Not conscious
  that you have been seeking
    suddenly
  you come upon it

the village in the Welsh hills
    dust free
  with no road out
but the one you came in by.

  A bird chimes
  from a green tree
the hour that is no hour
  you know. The river dawdles
to hold a mirror for you
where you may see yourself
  as you are, a traveller
    with the moon's halo
  above him, whom has arrived
  after long journeying where he
    began, catching this
  one truth by surprise
that there is everything to look forward to.

R. S. Thomas (1913–2000)

Epithalamion

LINES 1–13

Hark, hearer, hear what I do; lend a thought now,
   make believe
We are leaf-whelmed somewhere with the hood
Of some branchy bunchy bushybowered wood,
Southern dene or Lancashire clough or Devon cleave,
That leans along the loins of hills, where a
   candycoloured, where a gluegold-brown
Marbled river, boisterously beautiful, between
Roots and rocks is danced and dandled, all in froth and
   waterblowballs, down.
We are there, when we hear a shout
That the hanging honeysuck, the dogeared hazels in the
   cover
Makes dither, makes hover
And the riot of a rout
Of, it must be, boys from the town
Bathing: it is summer's sovereign good.

Gerard Manley Hopkins (1844–1889)

The Green Pigeon

O Flutterer of green, amid green leaves,
Is it joy, pure joy, makes you whistle like a boy,
Knowing half a tune he never quite achieves?

O Learner of a wistful melody,
I can hear your quaint refrain, lilting down and up again,
Where you crouch among the leaves half-hid from me.

O Teacher of a woodland harmony,
I can see your colours blend with the leaves, and without end
Through my heart there runs the tune you taught to me.

John Still (1880–1941)

The Lake Isle of Innisfree

I will arise and go now, and go to Innisfree,
And a small cabin build there, of clay and wattles made:
Nine bean-rows will I have there, a hive for the
   honey bee,
And live alone in a bee-loud glade.

And I shall have some peace there, for peace comes
   dropping slow,
Dropping from the veils of morning to where the
   cricket sings;
There midnight's all a glimmer, and noon a purple glow,
And evening full of the linnet's wings.

I will arise and go now, for always night and day
I hear lake water lapping with low sounds by the shore;
While I stand on the roadway, or on the pavements grey,
I hear it in the deep heart's core.

W. B. Yeats (1865–1939)

The Girl with the Ball

She ran with her ball in her light dress floating and free,
Tossing it, tossing it up in the evening light,
She ran with her ball at the edge of the outgoing sea
On sand which the dropping sun turned bright.

Over the sea hung birds more white than the skin
Of the last few swimmers who took the waves with their
  breasts;
The birds dipped straight as her ball when a silver fin
Glanced in the shallow crests.

She ran so swift, and suddenly stopped as swift
To look at a shell, or splash up a pool in rain;
Wind blew, and she in the wind began to drift
Foam-like, and suddenly ran again.

Children who played on the shore in the last of the day
Paused and watched in wonder her rise and fall
Like elders watching a child: she was younger than they
As she ran by the sea with her ball.

Her hair was loose and she had no shoes on her feet,
And her image ran under her feet on the wet gold shore,
She threw up her ball and she caught it, and once
  laughed sweet
As though the world had never heard laughter before.

Eleanor Farjeon (1881–1965)

To Lilly

Right merry lass, thy overweening joy
Turns an old man into a merry boy.
One hour with thee pays off the long arrears,
The heavy debt of almost fifty years.
Oft have I view'd that lake so beautiful,
And felt its quiet power, benign, to lull
The inward being to a soft repose;
Patient, yet not forgetful of the woes
That are the heritage of mortal breath,
As if one note divided life and death.
But thou, sweet maid, with ready mirth dost fill
The wide survey of water, wood, and hill.
I feel a pulse of pleasure newly born.
And scarce believe that 'man was made to mourn'.

Hartley Coleridge (1796–1849)

Afternoon on a Hill

I will be the gladdest thing
　　Under the sun!
I will touch a hundred flowers
　　And not pick one.

I will look at cliffs and clouds
　　With quiet eyes,
Watch the wind bow down the grass,
　　And the grass rise.

And when lights begin to show
　　Up from the town,
I will mark which must be mine,
　　And then start down!

Edna St Vincent Millay (1892–1950)

The Butterfly's Ball and the Grasshopper's Feast

VERSES 1 AND 2

Come take up your hats and away let us haste
To the Butterfly's ball and the Grasshopper's feast.
The trumpeter Gad-fly has summoned the crew,
And the revels are now only waiting for you.

On the smooth shaven grass by the side of the wood,
Beneath a broad oak that for ages has stood,
See the children of earth and the tenants of air,
For an evening's amusement together repair.

Thomas Roscoe (1791–1871)

August

For August, be your dwelling thirty towers
   Within an Alpine valley mountainous,
    Where never the sea-wind may vex your house,
But clear life separate, like a star, be yours.
There horses shall wait saddled at all hours,
   That ye may mount at morning or at eve:
    On each hand either ridge ye shall perceive,
A mile apart, which soon a good beast scours.
So alway, drawing homewards, ye shall tread
   Your valley parted by a rivulet
    Which day and night shall flow sedate and smooth.
There all through noon ye may possess the shade,
   And there your open purses shall entreat
    The best of Tuscan cheer to feed your youth.

Folgóre da San Gimignano (c. 1270–c. 1332)
Translated by Dante Gabriel Rossetti (1828–1882)

Farewell

FROM *DOVER TO MUNICH*

Farewell, farewell! Before our prow
   Leaps in white foam the noisy channel,
A tourist's cap is on my brow,
   My legs are cased in tourists' flannel:

Around me gasp the invalids –
   The quantity to-night is fearful –
I take a brace or so of weeds,
   And feel (as yet) extremely cheerful.

The night wears on: – my thirst I quench
   With one imperial pint of porter;
Then drop upon a casual bench –
   (The bench is short, but I am shorter) –

Place 'neath my head the *harve-sac*
   Which I have stowed my little all in,
And sleep, though moist about the back,
   Serenely in an old tarpaulin.

C. S. Calverley (1831–1884)

Holiday at Hampton Court

Scales of pearly cloud inlay
  North and south the turquoise sky,
While the diamond lamp of day
  Quenchless burns, and time on high
A moment halts upon his way
  Bidding noon again good-bye.

Gaffers, gammers, huzzies, louts,
  Couples, gangs, and families
Sprawling, shake, with Babel-shouts
  Bluff King Hal's funereal trees;
And eddying groups of stare-abouts
  Quiz the sandstone Hercules.

When their tongues and tempers tire,
  Harry and his little lot
Condescendingly admire
  Lozenge-bed and crescent-plot,
Aglow with links of azure fire,
  Pansy and forget-me-not.

Where the emerald shadows rest
  In the lofty woodland aisle,
Chaffing lovers quaintly dressed
  Chase and double many a mile,
Indifferent exiles in the west
  Making love in cockney style.

Now the echoing palace fills;
  Men and women, girls and boys
Trample past the swords and frills,
  Kings and Queens and trulls and toys;
Or listening loll on window-sills,
  Happy amateurs of noise!

That for pictured rooms of state!
  Out they hurry, wench and knave,
Where beyond the palace-gate
  Dusty legions swarm and rave,
With laughter, shriek, inane debate,
  Kentish fire and comic stave.

Voices from the river call;
  Organs hammer tune on tune;
Larks triumphant over all
  Herald twilight coming soon,
For as the sun begins to fall
  Near the zenith gleams the moon.

John Davidson (1857–1909)

High Summer

I never wholly feel that summer is high,
However green the trees, or loud the birds,
However movelessly eye winking herds,
Stand in field ponds, or under large trees lie, –
Till I do climb all cultured pastures by,
That hedged by hedgerows studiously fretted trim,
Smile like a lady's face with lace laced prim,
And on some moor or hill that seeks the sky
Lonely and nakedly, – utterly lie down,
And feel the sunshine throbbing on body and limb,
My drowsy brain in pleasant drunkenness swim,
Each rising thought sink back, and dreamily drown,
Smiles creep o'er my face, and smother my lips, and cloy,
Each muscle sink to itself, and separately enjoy.

Ebenezer Jones (1820–1860)

The Catch

Forget
the long, smouldering
afternoon. It is

this moment
when the ball scoots
off the edge

of the bat; upwards,
backwards, falling
seemingly

beyond him
yet he reaches
and picks it

out
of its loop
like

an apple
from a branch,
the first of the season.

Simon Armitage (1963–)

On the Sussex Downs

Over the downs there were birds flying,
 Far off glittered the sea,
And toward the north the weald of Sussex
 Lay like a kingdom under me.

I was happier than the larks
 That nest on the downs and sing to the sky –
Over the downs the birds flying
 Were not so happy as I.

It was not you, though you were near,
 Though you were good to hear and see,
It was not earth, it was not heaven,
 It was myself that sang in me.

Sara Teasdale (1884–1933)

The Scholar Gipsy

VERSES I–III

Go, for they call you, shepherd, from the hill;
  Go, shepherd, and untie the wattled cotes!
    No longer leave thy wistful flock unfed,
  Nor let thy bawling fellows rack their throats,
    Nor the cropp'd herbage shoot another head.
      But when the fields are still,
  And the tired men and dogs all gone to rest,
    And only the white sheep are sometimes seen
    Cross and recross the strips of moon-blanch'd green,
Come, shepherd, and again begin the quest!

Here, where the reaper was at work of late –
  In this high field's dark corner, where he leaves
    His coat, his basket, and his earthen cruse,
  And in the sun all morning binds the sheaves,
    Then here, at noon, comes back his stores to use –
      Here will I sit and wait,
  While to my ear from uplands far away
    The bleating of the folded flocks is borne,
    With distant cries of reapers in the corn –
All the live murmur of a summer's day.

Screen'd is this nook o'er the high, half-reap'd field,
  And here till sun-down, shepherd! will I be.
    Through the thick corn the scarlet poppies peep,
  And round green roots and yellowing stalks I see
    Pale pink convolvulus in tendrils creep;
      And air-swept lindens yield
  Their scent, and rustle down their perfumed showers
    Of bloom on the bent grass where I am laid,
    And bower me from the August sun with shade;
  And the eye travels down to Oxford's towers.

Matthew Arnold (1822–1888)

Men on Allotments

As mute as monks, tidy as bachelors,
They manicure their little plots of earth.
Pop music from the council house estate
Counterpoints with the Sunday-morning bells,
But neither siren voice has power for these
Drab solitary men who spend their time
Kneeling, or fetching water, soberly,
Or walking softly down a row of beans.

Like drill-sergeants, they measure their recruits.
The infant sprig receives the proper space
The manly fullgrown cauliflower will need.
And all must toe the line here; stern and leaf,
As well as root, obey the rule of string.
Domesticated tilth aligns itself
In sweet conformity; but head in air
Soars the unruly loveliness of beans.

They visit hidden places of the earth
When tenderly with fork and hand they grope
To lift potatoes, and the round, flushed globes
Tumble like pearls out of the moving soil.
They share strange intuitions, know how much
Patience and energy and sense of poise
It takes to be an onion; and they share
The subtle benediction of the beans.

They see the casual holiness that spreads
Along obedient furrows. Cabbages
Unfurl their veined and rounded fans in joy,
And buds of sprouts rejoice along their stalks.
The ferny tops of carrots, stout red stems
Of beetroot, zany sunflowers with blond hair
And bloodshot faces, shine like seraphim
Under the long flat fingers of the beans.

U. A. Fanthorpe (1929–2009)

The Guinea Pigs' Garden

We have a little garden,
   A garden of our own,
And every day we water there
   The seeds that we have sown.

We love our little garden,
   And tend it with such care,
You will not find a faded leaf
   Or blighted blossom there.

Beatrix Potter (1866–1943)

Dinner

FROM *STOCKLEWATH; OR, THE CUMBRIAN VILLAGE*
LINES 37–56

But now the sun's bright whirling wheels appear
On the broad front of noon, in full career,
A sign more welcome hangs not in the air,
For now the sister's call the brothers hear;
Dinner's the word, and every cave around
Devours the voice, and feasts upon the sound.
''Tis dinner, father!' all the brothers cry,
Throw down the spade, and heave the pickaxe by;
''Tis dinner, father!' Home they panting go,
While the tired parent still pants on more slow.
Now the fried rasher meets them on the way,
And savoury pancakes welcome steams convey.
Their pace they mend, till at the pump they stand,
Deluge the face, and purify the hand,
And then to dinner. There the women wait,
And the tired father fills his chair of state;
Smoking potatoes meet their thankful eyes,
And Hunger wafts the grateful sacrifice;
To her libations of sweet milk are pour'd,
And Peace and Plenty watch around the board.

Susanna Blamire (1747–1794)

What Harvest Halfe so Sweet is

What harvest halfe so sweet is,
As still to reape the kisses
   Growne ripe in sowing?
And straight to be receiver
Of that which thou art giver,
   Rich in bestowing?
Kisse then, my harvest Queene,
   Full garners heaping;
Kisses, ripest when th' are greene,
   Want onely reaping.

The Dove alone expresses
Her fervencie in kisses,
   Of all most loving:
A creature as offencelesse
As those things that are sencelesse
   And void of moving.
Let us so love and kisse,
   Though all envie us:
That which kinde, and harmlesse is,
   None can denie us.

Thomas Campion (1567–1620)

Chamber Music: I

Strings in the earth and air
  Make music sweet;
Strings by the river where
  The willows meet.

There's music along the river
  For Love wanders there,
Pale flowers on his mantle,
  Dark leaves on his hair.

All softly playing,
  With head to the music bent,
And fingers straying
  Upon an instrument.

James Joyce (1882–1941)

A Subaltern's Love-song

Miss J. Hunter Dunn, Miss J. Hunter Dunn,
Furnish'd and burnish'd by Aldershot sun,
What strenuous singles we played after tea,
We in the tournament – you against me!

Love-thirty, love-forty, oh! weakness of joy,
The speed of a swallow, the grace of a boy,
With carefullest carelessness, gaily you won,
I am weak from your loveliness, Joan Hunter Dunn.

Miss Joan Hunter Dunn, Miss Joan Hunter Dunn,
How mad I am, sad I am, glad that you won,
The warm-handled racket is back in its press,
But my shock-headed victor, she loves me no less.

Her father's euonymus shines as we walk,
And swing past the summer-house, buried in talk,
And cool the verandah that welcomes us in
To the six-o'clock news and a lime juice and gin.

The scent of the conifers, sound of the bath,
The view from my bedroom of moss-dappled path,
As I struggle with double-end evening tie,
For we dance at the Golf Club, my victor and I.

On the floor of her bedroom lie blazer and shorts
And the cream-coloured walls are be-trophied with sports,
And westering, questioning settles the sun
On your low-leaded window, Miss Joan Hunter Dunn.

The Hillman is waiting, the light's in the hall,
The pictures of Egypt are bright on the wall,
My sweet, I am standing beside the oak stair
And there on the landing's the light on your hair.

By roads 'not adopted', by woodlanded ways,
She drove to the club in the late summer haze,
Into nine-o'clock Camberley, heavy with bells
And mushroomy, pine-woody, evergreen smells.

Miss Joan Hunter Dunn, Miss Joan Hunter Dunn,
I can hear from the car-park the dance has begun.
Oh! full Surrey twilight! importunate band!
Oh! strongly adorable tennis-girl's hand.

Around us are Rovers and Austins afar,
Above us, the intimate roof of the car,
And here on my right is the girl of my choice,
With the tilt of her nose and the chime of her voice,

And the scent of her wrap, and the words never said,
And the ominous, ominous dancing ahead.
We sat in the car park till twenty to one
And now I'm engaged to Miss Joan Hunter Dunn.

John Betjeman (1906-1984)

Prelude

FROM *VOICES OF THE NIGHT*, VERSES 1–4

Pleasant it was, when woods were green
   And winds were soft and low,
To lie amid some sylvan scene,
Where, the long drooping boughs between,
Shadows dark and sunlight sheen
   Alternate come and go;

Or where the denser grove receives
   No sunlight from above,
But the dark foliage interweaves
In one unbroken roof of leaves,
Underneath whose sloping eaves
   The shadows hardly move.

Beneath some patriarchal tree
   I lay upon the ground;
His hoary arms uplifted he,
And all the broad leaves over me
Clapped their little hands in glee,
   With one continuous sound; –

A slumberous sound, a sound that brings
   The feelings of a dream,
As of innumerable wings,
As, when a bell no longer swings,
Faint the hollow murmur rings
   O'er meadow, lake, and stream.

Henry Wadsworth Longfellow (1807–1882)

Contentment

I'm glad the sky is painted blue:
And the earth is painted green:
And such a lot of nice fresh air
All sandwiched in between.

E. C. Bentley (1875–1956)

Rose-cheekt Lawra

FROM *OBSERVATIONS IN THE ART OF ENGLISH POESIE*

Rose-cheekt *Lawra*, come,
Sing thou smoothly with thy beawties
Silent musick, either other
      Sweetely gracing.
Lovely formes do flowe
From concent divinely framed;
Heav'n is musick, and thy beawties
      Birth is heavenly.
These dull notes we sing
Discords neede for helps to grace them;
Only beawty purely loving
      Knowes no discord,
But still mooves delight,
Like cleare springs renu'd by flowing,
Ever perfect, ever in them –
      selves eternall.

Thomas Campion (1567–1620)

Morris Dancers

Deckt out in ribbons gay and papers cut
Fine as a maidens fancy off they strut
And act the morris dance from door to door
Their highest gains a penny nothing more
The children leave their toys to see them play
And laughing maidens lay their work away
The stolen apple in her apron lies
To give her lover in his gay disguise
Een the old woman leaves her knitting off
And lays the bellows in her lap to laugh
Upon the floor the stool made waggons lie
And playing scholars lay the lesson bye
The cat and dog in wonder run away
And hide beneath the table from the fray

John Clare (1793–1864)

An Anniversary

HE

Bright, my belovèd, be thy day,
  This eve of Summer's fall:
And Autumn mass his flowers gay
  To crown thy festival!

SHE

I care not if the morn be bright,
  Living in thy love-rays:
No flower I need for my delight,
  Being crownèd with thy praise.

HE

O many years and joyfully
  This sun to thee return;
Ever all men speak well of thee,
  Nor any angel mourn!

SHE

For length of life I would not pray,
  If thy life were to seek;
Nor ask what men and angels say
  But when of thee they speak.

HE

Arise! The sky hath heard my song,
  The flowers o'erhear thy praise;
And little loves are waking long
  To wish thee happy days.

Robert Bridges (1844–1930)

SEPTEMBER

My Spirit is Soaring

The Little Hill

This is the hill, ringed by the misty shire –
The mossy, southern hill,
The little hill where larches climb so high.
Among the stars aslant
They chant;
Along the purple lower slopes they lie
In lazy golden smoke, more faint, more still
Than the pale woodsmoke of the cottage fire.
Here some calm Presence takes me by the hand
And all my heart is lifted by the chant
Of them that lean aslant
In golden smoke, and sing, and softly bend:
And out from every larch-bole steals a friend.

Mary Webb (1881–1927)

On the Picture of Two Dolphins in a Fountayne

These dolphins twisting each on either side
For joy leapt upp, and gazing there abide;
And whereas other waters fish doe bring,
Here from the fishes doe the waters spring,
Who think it is more glorious to give
Than to receive the juice whereby they live:
And by this milk-white bason learne you may
That pure hands you should bring or beare away,
For which the bason wants no furniture,
Each dolphin wayting makes his mouth an ewer,
Your welcome then you well may understand
When fish themselves give water to your hand.

William Strode (c. 1602–1643)

Composed Upon Westminster Bridge, September 3, 1802

WRITTEN ON THE ROOF OF A COACH, ON MY WAY TO FRANCE

Earth has not anything to show more fair:
Dull would he be of soul who could pass by
A sight so touching in its majesty:
This City now doth, like a garment, wear
The beauty of the morning; silent, bare,
Ships, towers, domes, theatres, and temples lie
Open unto the fields, and to the sky;
All bright and glittering in the smokeless air.
Never did sun more beautifully steep
In his first splendour, valley, rock, or hill;
Ne'er saw I, never felt, a calm so deep!
The river glideth at his own sweet will:
Dear God! the very houses seem asleep;
And all that mighty heart is lying still!

William Wordsworth (1770–1850)

The Land of Lost Content

A SHROPSHIRE LAD XL

Into my heart an air that kills
  From yon far country blows:
What are those blue remembered hills,
  What spires, what farms are those?

That is the land of lost content,
  I see it shining plain,
The happy highways where I went
  And cannot come again.

A. E. Housman (1859–1936)

Thanks in Old Age

Thanks in old age – thanks ere I go,
For health, the midday sun, the impalpable air – for life,
    mere life,
For precious ever-lingering memories, (of you my
    mother dear – you, father – you, brothers, sisters,
    friends,)
For all my days – not those of peace alone – the days of
    war the same,
For gentle words, caresses, gifts from foreign lands,
For shelter, wine and meat – for sweet appreciation,
(You distant, dim unknown – or young or old –
    countless, unspecified, readers belov'd,
We never met, and ne'er shall meet – and yet our souls
    embrace, long, close and long;)
For beings, groups, love, deeds, words, books – for
    colors, forms,
For all the brave strong men – devoted, hardy men –
    who've forward sprung in freedom's help, all years, all
    lands,
For braver, stronger, more devoted men – (a special
    laurel ere I go, to life's war's chosen ones,
The cannoneers of song and thought – the great
    artillerists – the foremost leaders, captains of the soul:)
As soldier from an ended war return'd – As traveler out
    of myriads, to the long procession retrospective,
Thanks – joyful thanks! – a soldier's, traveler's thanks.

Walt Whitman (1819–1892)

Fruit for All

FROM *TO PENSHURST*, LINES 39–44

Then hath thy orchard fruit, thy garden flowers,
Fresh as the air, and new as are the houres.
The earely cherry, with the later plum,
Fig, grape, and quince, each in his time doth come;
The blushing apricot and woolly peach
Hang on thy walls, that every child may reach.

Ben Jonson (1572–1637)

Living

Slow bleak awakening from the morning dream
Brings me in contact with the sudden day.
I am alive – this I.
I let my fingers move along my body.
Realization warns them, and my nerves
Prepare their rapid messages and signals.
While Memory begins recording, coding,
Repeating; all the time Imagination
Mutters: You'll only die.

Here's a new day. O Pendulum move slowly!
My usual clothes are waiting on their peg.
I am alive – this I.
And in a moment Habit, like a crane,
Will bow its neck and dip its pulleyed cable,
Gathering me, my body, and our garment,
And swing me forth, oblivious of my question,
Into the daylight – why?

I think of all the others who awaken,
And wonder if they go to meet the morning
More valiantly than I;
Nor asking of this Day they will be living:
What have I done that I should be alive?
O, can I not forget that I am living?
How shall I reconcile the two conditions:
Living, and yet – to die?

Between the curtains the autumnal sunlight
With lean and yellow finger points me out;
The clock moans: Why? Why? Why?
But suddenly, as if without a reason,
Heart, Brain, and Body, and Imagination
All gather in tumultuous joy together,
Running like children down the path of morning
To fields where they can play without a quarrel:
A country I'd forgotten, but remember,
And welcome with a cry.

O cool glad pasture; living tree, tall corn,
Great cliff, or languid sloping sand, cold sea,
Waves; rivers curving; you, eternal flowers,
Give me content, while I can think of you:
Give me your living breath!
Back to your rampart, Death.

Harold Monro (1879–1932)

Songs of Travel

VERSE IX

Let Beauty awake in the morn from beautiful dreams,
　　　Beauty awake from rest!
　　　Let Beauty awake
　　　For Beauty's sake
In the hour when the birds awake in the brake
　　　And the stars are bright in the west!

Let Beauty awake in the eve from the slumber of day,
　　　Awake in the crimson eve!
　　　In the day's dusk end
　　　When the shades ascend,
Let her wake to the kiss of a tender friend
　　　To render again and receive!

Robert Louis Stevenson (1850–1894)

The Garden

VERSES 5–7

v

What wond'rous Life is this I lead!
Ripe Apples drop about my head;
The Luscious Clusters of the Vine
Upon my Mouth do crush their Wine;
The Nectaren, and curious Peach,
Into my hands themselves do reach;
Stumbling on Melons, as I pass,
Insnar'd with Flow'rs, I fall on Grass.

vi

Mean while the Mind, from pleasures less,
Withdraws into its happiness:
The Mind, that Ocean where each kind
Does streight its own resemblance find;
Yet it creates, transcending these,
Far other Worlds, and other Seas;
Annihilating all that's made
To a green Thought in a green Shade.

vii

Here at the Fountains sliding foot,
Or at some Fruit-tree's mossy root,
Casting the Bodies Vest aside,
My Soul into the boughs does glide:
There like a bird it sits, and sings,
Then whets, and combs its silver Wings;
And, till prepar'd for longer flight,
Waves in its Plumes the various Light.

Andrew Marvell (1621–1678)

The Human Touch

'Tis the human touch in this world that counts,
  The touch of your hand and mine,
Which means far more to the fainting heart
  Than shelter and bread and wine;
For shelter is gone when the night is o'er,
  And bread lasts only a day.
But the touch of the hand and the sound of the voice
  Sing on in the soul alway.

Spencer Michael Free (1856–1938)

Ode to Happiness

LINES 1–21

Spirit, that rarely comest now
　And only to contrast my gloom,
　Like rainbow-feathered birds that bloom
A moment on some autumn bough
That, with the spurn of their farewell
Sheds its last leaves, – thou once didst dwell
　With me year-long, and make intense
To boyhood's wisely vacant days
Their fleet but all-sufficing grace
　Of trustful inexperience,
　While soul could still transfigure sense,
And thrill, as with love's first caress,
At life's mere unexpectedness.
　Days when my blood would leap and run
　　As full of sunshine as a breeze,
　　Or spray tossed up by Summer seas
　That doubts if it be sea or sun!
Days that flew swiftly like the band
　That played in Grecian games at strife,
And passed from eager hand to hand
　The onward-dancing torch of life!

James Russell Lowell (1819–1891)

Home Sweet Home

'Mid pleasures and palaces though we may roam,
   Be it ever so humble, there's no place like home!
A charm from the sky seems to hallow us there,
   Which, seek through the world, is ne'er met
     with elsewhere!
      Home, Home, Sweet, Sweet Home!
      There's no place like Home!
      There's no place like Home!

An exile from home, splendor dazzles in vain!
   Oh, give me my lowly thatched cottage again!
The birds singing gayly, that came at my call –
   Give me them! – and the peace of mind, dearer than all!
      Home, Home, Sweet, Sweet Home!
      There's no place like Home!
      There's no place like Home!

John Howard Payne (1791–1852)

A Greeting

Good morning, Life, – and all
Things glad and beautiful.
My pockets nothing hold,
But he that owns the gold,
The Sun, is my great friend –
His spending has no end.

Hail to the morning sky,
Which bright clouds measure high;
Hail to you birds whose throats
Would number leaves by notes;
Hail to you shady bowers,
And you green fields of flowers.

Hail to you women fair,
That make a show so rare
In cloth as white as milk –
Be't calico or silk:
Good morning, Life – and all
Things glad and beautiful.

W. H. Davies (1871–1940)

Jacke and Jone

Jacke and *Jone* they thinke no ill,
But loving live, and merry still;
Doe their week dayes worke, and pray
Devotely on the holy day;
Skip and trip it on the greene,
And help to chuse the Summer Queene;
Lash out, at a Country Feast,
Their silver penny with the best.

Well can they judge of nappy Ale,
And tell at large a Winter tale;
Climbe up to the Apple loft,
And turne the Crabs till they be soft.
Tib is all the fathers joy,
And little *Tom* the mothers boy.
All their pleasure is Content;
And care, to pay their yearely rent.

Jone can call by name her Cowes,
And decke her windows with greene boughs;
Shee can wreathes and tuttyes make,
And trimme with plums a Bridall Cake.
Jacke knows what brings gaine or losse;
And his long Flaile can stoutly tosse;
Makes the hedge, which others breake;
And ever thinkes what he doth speake.

Now, you Courtly Dames and Knights,
That study onely strange delights,
Though you scorne the home-spun gray,
And revell in your rich array;
Though your tongues dissemble deepe,
And can your heads from danger keepe;
Yet, for all your pompe and traine,
Securer lives the silly Swaine.

Thomas Campion (1567–1620)

Pied Beauty

Glory be to God for dappled things –
　　For skies of couple-colour as a brinded cow;
　　　　For rose-moles all in stipple upon trout that swim;
Fresh-firecoal chestnut-falls; finches' wings;
　　Landscape plotted and pierced – fold, fallow, and plough;
　　　　And áll trádes, their gear and tackle and trim.

All things counter, original, spare, strange;
　　Whatever is fickle, freckled (who knows how?)
　　With swift, slow; sweet, sour; adazzle, dim;
He fathers-forth whose beauty is past change:
　　　　Praise him.

Gerard Manley Hopkins (1844–1889)

Dancing

I cannot dance in a stuffy room
   To the music of a ball;
Indoors where lights and people are
   I cannot dance at all.

But out on the lawn of an afternoon
   Jane takes my hand, and we
Dance gayer than all the poplar leaves,
   Or ships on a windy sea.

Rachel Field (1894–1942)

Edinburgh Stroll

I leave the Tollcross traffic and walk by the Meadows
between two rows of trees, all looking
as grave as Elders of the Kirk – but
wait till the wind blows.

Dogs are hunting for smells. A few men
are practicing approach shots
on the dwarfish golf course. Some children
are incomprehensibly playing.

And between two heaps of jackets
a boy scores a goal –
the best one ever.

Past the infirmary I go back to the traffic
cross it, and there's Sandy Bell's Bar.

Tollcross to Sandy Bell's Bar
a short walk with a long conclusion.

Norman MacCaig (1910–1996)

Lines Composed in a Wood on a Windy Day

My soul is awakened, my spirit is soaring,
And carried aloft on the wings of the breeze;
For, above, and around me, the wild wind is roaring
Arousing to rapture the earth and the seas.

The long withered grass in the sunshine is glancing,
The bare trees are tossing their branches on high;
The dead leaves beneath them are merrily dancing,
The white clouds are scudding across the blue sky.

I wish I could see how the ocean is lashing
The foam of its billows to whirlwinds of spray,
I wish I could see how its proud waves are dashing
And hear the wild roar of their thunder today!

Anne Brontë (1820–1849)

Meeting at Night

I

The grey sea and the long black land;
And the yellow half-moon large and low;
And the startled little waves that leap
In fiery ringlets from their sleep,
As I gain the cove with pushing prow,
And quench its speed in the slushy sand.

II

Then a mile of warm sea-scented beach;
Three fields to cross till a farm appears;
A tap at the pane, the quick sharp scratch
And blue spurt of a lighted match,
And a voice less loud, thro' its joys and fears,
Than the two hearts beating each to each!

Robert Browning (1812–1889)

Happy is the Man

PROVERBS, CHAPTER 3, VERSES 13–17

Happy is the man that findeth wisdom, and the
man that getteth understanding.
For the merchandise of it is better than the merchandise
of silver, and the gain thereof than fine gold.
She is more precious than rubies: and all the things thou
canst desire are not to be compared unto her.
Length of days is in her right hand; and in her left hand
riches and honour.
Her ways are ways of pleasantness, and all her
paths are peace.

The King James Bible

To Autumn

I

Season of mists and mellow fruitfulness,
  Close bosom-friend of the maturing sun;
Conspiring with him how to load and bless
  With fruit the vines that round the thatch-eves run;
To bend with apples the moss'd cottage-trees,
  And fill all fruit with ripeness to the core;
    To swell the gourd, and plump the hazel shells
  With a sweet kernel; to set budding more,
And still more, later flowers for the bees,
Until they think warm days will never cease,
    For Summer has o'er-brimmed their clammy cells.

II

Who hath not seen thee oft amid thy store?
  Sometimes whoever seeks abroad may find
Thee sitting careless on a granary floor,
  Thy hair soft-lifted by the winnowing wind;
Or on a half-reap'd furrow sound asleep,
  Drows'd with the fume of poppies, while thy hook
    Spares the next swathe and all its twined flowers:
And sometimes like a gleaner thou dost keep
  Steady thy laden head across a brook;
  Or by a cyder-press, with patient look,
    Thou watchest the last oozings hours by hours.

III

Where are the songs of Spring? Ay, where are they?
  Think not of them, thou hast thy music too, –
While barred clouds bloom the soft-dying day,
  And touch the stubble-plains with rosy hue;
Then in a wilful choir the small gnats mourn
  Among the river sallows, borne aloft
    Or sinking as the light wind lives or dies;
And full-grown lambs loud bleat from hilly bourn;
  Hedge-crickets sing; and now with treble soft
  The red-breast whistles from a garden-croft;
    And gathering swallows twitter in the skies.

John Keats (1795–1821)

Oh Happiness!

FROM *AN ESSAY ON MAN*, EPISTLE IV: OF THE NATURE AND STATE
OF MAN, WITH RESPECT TO HAPPINESS

Oh Happiness! our being's end and aim!
Good, Pleasure, Ease, Content! whate'er thy name,
That something still which prompts th' eternal sigh,
For which we bear to live, or dare to die,
Which still so near us, yet beyond us lies,
O'er-look'd, seen double, by the fool, and wise.
Plant of celestial seed! if dropt below,
Say in what mortal soil thou deign'st to grow?
Fair op'ning to some Court's propitious shine,
Or deep with di'monds in the flaming mine?
Twin'd with the wreaths Parnassian laurels yield,
Or reap'd in iron harvests of the field?
Where grows? – where grows it not? If vain our toil,
We ought to blame the culture, not the soil:
Fix'd to no spot is Happiness sincere,
'Tis nowhere to be found, or ev'rywhere;
'Tis never to be bought, but always free,
And fled from monarchs, St. John! dwells with thee.

Alexander Pope (1688–1744)

How Happy is the Little Stone

How happy is the little Stone
That rambles in the Road alone,
And doesn't care about Careers
And Exigencies never fears –
Whose Coat of elemental Brown
A passing Universe put on,
And independent as the Sun
Associates or glows alone,
Fulfilling absolute Decree
In casual simplicity –

Emily Dickinson (1830–1886)

Song from the Ship

FROM *DEATH'S JEST-BOOK*, ACT I, SCENE I

To sea, to sea! The calm is o'er;
   The wanton water leaps in sport,
And rattles down the pebbly shore;
   The dolphin wheels, the sea-cows snort,
And unseen Mermaids' pearly song
Comes bubbling up, the weeds among.
   Fling broad the sail, dip deep the oar:
   To sea, to sea! the calm is o'er.

To sea, to sea! our wide-winged bark
   Shall billowy cleave its sunny way,
And with its shadow, fleet and dark,
   Break the caved Tritons' azure day,
Like mighty eagle soaring light
O'er antelopes on Alpine height.
   The anchor heaves, the ship swings free,
   The sails swell full. To sea, to sea!

Thomas Lovell Beddoes (1803–1849)

The Long-Tailed Robin

Among the underbrush I hear you,
Softly piping, and so sweetly trilling,
While the darkening woods are slowly filling
With the melody that ever hovers near you,
Welling on, swelling on, as you sing, as you ring,
And now I hear the flutter of your wing,
While yet another thicket bursts in voice,
Tender and wistful tones that seem half sad,
Rounded and mellow notes that sound all glad,
And be you sad or glad I must rejoice
While your clear voice
Pours on, and still has powers
To sing the feelings of the silent flowers.

John Still (1880–1941)

Travelling

This is the spot: – how mildly does the sun
Shine in between the fading leaves! the air
In the habitual silence of this wood
Is more than silent: and this bed of heath,
Where shall we find so sweet a resting-place?
Come! – let me see thee sink into a dream
Of quiet thoughts, – protracted till thine eye
Be calm as water when the winds are gone
And no one can tell whither. – my sweet friend!
We two have had such happy hours together
That my heart melts in me to think of it.

William Wordsworth (1770–1850)

The Escape

I believe in the increasing of life: whatever
　　Leads to the seeing of small trifles,
Real, beautiful, is good and an act never
　　Is worthier than in freeing spirit that stifles
Under ingratitude's weight, nor is anything done
　　Wiselier than the moving or breaking to sight
Of a thing hidden under by custom; revealed,
　　Fulfilled, used (sound-fashioned) any way out to delight.
Trefoil – hedge sparrow – the stars on the edge at night.

Ivor Gurney (1890–1937)

Praises of a Country Life

VERSES 1-8

How blest is he who far from Cares,
  Like the old race of Men
His own paternal fields doth till
  Free from all wrongful gain,

To action he is neither roused
  By the harsh Trumpet's sound
Nor trembles at the angry sea
  Which rages all around.

He either joins the fruitful vine
  To the tall Poplar Tree,
Or feeding in a shady vale
  His wand'ring flock doth see

Or cutting off the useless bough
  More healthy plants he rears
Or pours fresh honey into jars
  Or Sheep so tender shears

But when adorned with Apples sweet
  Glad Autumn lifts his head
How he rejoices in the Pears
  And in the Grapes so red

With which, O Priapus, he thee
   Will bounteously reward
And thee, Sylvanus who doth well
   His territories guard.

Now in the shade he loves to lie
   Under the ancient Oak
And now upon the verdant grass
   Beneath th'o'erhanging rock

Meanwhile the dashing waters fall
   Birds in the forest sing
The little streamlets murmuring flow
   All which sweet slumbers bring.

Sara Coleridge (1802–1852)

Song

FROM *THE DOOM OF DEVORGOIL*

ACT 1, SCENE I, VERSES 1 AND 2

The sun upon the lake is low,
   The wild birds hush their song,
The hills have evening's deepest glow,
   Yet Leonard tarries long.
Now all whom varied toil and care
   From home and love divide,
In the calm sunset may repair
   Each to the loved ones side.

The noble dame, on turret high,
   Who waits her gallant knight,
Looks to the western beam to spy
   The flash of armour bright.
The village maid, with hand on brow
    The level ray to shade,
Upon the footpath watches now
   For Colin's darkening plaid.

Sir Walter Scott (1771–1832)

For an Autumn Festival

VERSES I–V

The Persian's flowery gifts, the shrine
   Of fruitful Ceres, charm no more;
The woven wreaths of oak and pine
   Are dust along the Isthmian shore.

But beauty hath its homage still,
   And nature holds us still in debt;
And woman's grace and household skill,
   And manhood's toil, are honoured yet.

And we, to-day, amidst our flowers
   And fruits, have come to own again
The blessings of the summer hours,
   The early and the latter rain;

To see our Father's hand once more
   Reverse for us the plenteous horn
Of autumn, filled and running o'er
   With fruit, and flower, and golden corn!

Once more the liberal year laughs out
   O'er richer stores than gems or gold;
Once more with harvest-song and shout
   Is Nature's bloodless triumph told.

John Greenleaf Whittier (1807–1892)

OCTOBER

The Golden Times

October

Give me October's meditative haze,
Its gossamer mornings, dewy-wimpled eves,
Dewy and fragrant, fragrant and secure,
The long slow sound of farmward-wending wains,
When homely Love sups quiet 'mid his sheaves,
Sups 'mid his sheaves, his sickle at his side,
And all is peace, peace and plump fruitfulness.

Alfred Austin (1835–1913)

My Heart Leaps Up

WRITTEN AT TOWN-END, GRASMERE

My heart leaps up when I behold
    A rainbow in the sky:
So it was when my life began;
So it is now I am a man;
So be it when I shall grow old,
    Or let me die!
The Child is father of the Man;
And I could wish my days to be
Bound each to each by natural piety.

William Wordsworth (1770–1850)

Opposite to Melancholy

Return, my joys, and hither bring
A tongue not made to speak but sing,
A jolly spleen, an inward feast,
A causeless laugh without a jest,
A face which gladness doth anoint,
An arm that springs out of his joint,
A sprightful gait that leaves no print,
And makes a feather of a flint,
A heart that's lighter than the air,
An eye still dancing in his sphere,
Strong mirth which nothing can control,
A body nimbler than the soul,
Free wandering thoughts not tied to muse,
Which think on all things, nothing choose,
Which ere we see them come are gone;
These life itself doth feed upon.

William Strode (c. 1602–1643)

Sunset

There is a band of dull gold in the west, and say
  what you like
again and again some god of evening leans out of it
and shares being with me, silkily
all of twilight.

D. H. Lawrence (1885–1930)

The World

VERSE I

I saw Eternity the other night,
Like a great *Ring* of pure and endless light,
   All calm, as it was bright;
And round beneath it, Time in hours, days, years,
      Driv'n by the spheres
Like a vast shadow mov'd, In which the world
   And all her train were hurl'd;
The doting Lover in his quaintest strain
      Did their Complain,
Near him, his Lute, his fancy, and his flights,
      Wits sour delights,
With gloves, and knots the silly snares of pleasure,
      Yet his dear Treasure
All scatter'd lay, while he his eys did pour
      Upon a flowr.

Henry Vaughan (1621–1695)

Dog

You little friend, your nose is ready; you sniff,
Asking for that expected walk,
(Your nostrils full of the happy rabbit-whiff)
And almost talk.

And so the moment becomes a moving force;
Coats glide down from their pegs in the humble dark;
You scamper the stairs,
Your body informed with the scent and the track
   and the mark
Of stoats and weasels, moles and badgers and hares.

We are going *Out.* You know the pitch of the word,
Probing the tone of thought as it comes through fog
And reaches by devious means (half-smelt, half-heard)
The four-legged brain of a walk-ecstatic dog.

Out in the garden your head is already low.
You are going your walk, you know,
And your limbs will draw
Joy from the earth through the touch of your padded paw.

Now, sending a little look to us behind,
Who follow slowly the track of your lovely play,
You carry our bodies forward away from mind
Into the light and fun of your useless day.

*

Thus, for your walk, we took ourselves, and went
Out by the hedge and the tree, to the open ground.
You ran, in delightful strata of wafted scent,
Over the hill without seeing the view;
Beauty hinted through primitive smell to you:
And that ultimate Beauty you track but rarely found.

Home ... and further joy will be surely there:
Supper full of the lovely taste of bone.
You lift up your nose again, and sniff, and stare
For the rapture known

Of the quick wild gorge of food and the still lie-down
While your people talk above you in the light
Of candles, and your dreams will merge and drown
Into the bed-delicious hours of night.

Harold Monro (1879–1932)

O Sweet Delight

O sweet delight, O more than human blisse,
With her to live that ever loving is;
To hear her speake, whose words are so well plac't,
That she by them, as they in her are grac't;
   Those lookes to view, that feast the viewers eye,
   How blest is he that may so live and dye!

Such love as this the golden times did know,
When all did reape, yet none tooke care to sow:
Such love as this an endlesse Summer makes,
And all distaste from fraile affection takes.
   So lov'd, so blest, in my belov'd am I;
   Which till their eyes ake, let yron men envy!

Thomas Campion (1567–1620)

All's Well

The clouds, which rise with thunder, slake
   Our thirsty souls with rain;
The blow most dreaded falls to break
   From off our limbs a chain;
And wrongs of man to man but make
   The love of God more plain.
As through the shadowy lens of even
The eye looks farthest into heaven
On gleams of star and depths of blue
The glaring sunshine never knew!

John Greenleaf Whittier (1807–1892)

Song

FROM *PROMETHEUS UNBOUND*, ACT II, SCENE V

My soul is an enchanted boat,
    Which, like a sleeping swan, doth float
Upon the silver waves of thy sweet singing;
And thine doth like an angel sit
    Beside the helm conducting it,
Whilst all the winds with melody are ringing.
    It seems to float ever, for ever,
    Upon that many-winding river,
    Between mountains, woods, abysses,
    A paradise of wildernesses!
Till, like one in slumber bound,
Borne to the ocean, I float down, around,
Into a sea profound, of ever-spreading sound:
    Meanwhile thy spirit lifts its pinions
    In music's most serene dominions;
Catching the winds that fan that happy heaven.
    And we sail on, away, afar,
    Without a course, without a star,
But, by the instinct of sweet music driven;
    Till through Elysian garden islets
    By thee, most beautiful of pilots,
    Where never mortal pinnace glided,
    The boat of my desire is guided:
Realms where the air we breathe is love,
Which in the winds on the waves doth move,
Harmonizing this earth with what we feel above.

Percy Bysshe Shelley (1792–1822)

Young Men Dancing, and the Old

Young men dancing, and the old
Sporting I with joy behold;
But an old man gay and free
Dancing most I love to see;
Age and youth alike he shares,
For his heart belies his hairs.

Thomas Stanley (1625–1678)

A Recipe

FROM *THE GONDOLIERS*

Take a pair of sparkling eyes,
  Hidden, ever and anon,
    In a merciful eclipse –
Do not heed their mild surprise –
  Having passed the Rubicon.
    Take a pair of rosy lips;
Take a figure trimly planned –
  Such as admiration whets –
    (Be particular in this);
Take a tender little hand,
  Fringed with dainty fingerettes,
    Press it – in parenthesis; –
Take all these, you lucky man –
Take and keep them, if you can!

Take a pretty little cot –
  Quite a miniature affair –
    Hung about with trellised vine,
Furnish it upon the spot
  With the treasures rich and rare
    I've endeavoured to define.
Live to love and love to live –
  You will ripen at your ease,
    Growing on the sunny side –
Fate has nothing more to give.
  You're a dainty man to please
    If you are not satisfied.
Take my counsel, happy man;
Act upon it, if you can!

W. S. Gilbert (1836–1911)

The Garden

VERSES 1–2

i

How vainly men themselves amaze
To win the Palm, the Oke or Bayes,
And their uncessant Labours see
Crown'd from some single Herb or Tree,
Whose short and narrow verged Shade
Does prudently their Toyles upbraid,
While all Flow'rs and all Trees do close
To weave the Garlands of repose.

ii

Fair quiet, have I found thee here,
And Innocence, thy Sister dear!
Mistaken long, I sought you then
In busie Companies of Men.
Your sacred Plants, if here below,
Only among the Plants will grow.
Society is all but rude,
To this delicious Solitude.

Andrew Marvell (1621–1678)

To-Night

Harry, you know at night
The larks in Castle Alley
Sing from the attic's height
As if the electric light
Were the true sun above a summer valley:
Whistle, don't knock, to-night.

I shall come early, Kate:
And we in Castle Alley
Will sit close out of sight
Alone, and ask no light
Of lamp or sun above a summer valley:
To-night I can stay late.

Edward Thomas (1878–1917)

A Birthday

My heart is like a singing bird
   Whose nest is in a watered shoot;
My heart is like an apple-tree
   Whose boughs are bent with thickset fruit;
My heart is like a rainbow shell
   That paddles in a halcyon sea;
My heart is gladder than all these
   Because my love is come to me.

Raise me a dais of silk and down;
   Hang it with vair and purple dyes;
Carve it in doves and pomegranates,
   And peacocks with a hundred eyes;
Work it in gold and silver grapes,
   In leaves and silver fleurs-de-lys;
Because the birthday of my life
   Is come, my love is come to me.

Christina Rossetti (1830–1894)

The Floor of Heaven

FROM *THE MERCHANT OF VENICE*, ACT V, SCENE I

Sit, Jessica. Look how the floor of heaven
Is thick inlaid with patens of bright gold.
There's not the smallest orb which thou behold'st
But in his motion like an angel sings,
Still choiring to the young-eyed cherubins.

William Shakespeare (1564–1616)

How Pleasant to Know ...

'How pleasant to know Mr. Lear!'
    Who has written such volumes of stuff!
Some think him ill-tempered and queer,
    But a few think him pleasant enough.

His mind is concrete and fastidious,
    His nose is remarkably big;
His visage is more or less hideous,
    His beard it resembles a wig.

He has ears, and two eyes, and ten fingers,
    Leastways if you reckon two thumbs;
Long ago he was one of the singers,
    But now he is one of the dumbs.

He sits in a beautiful parlour,
    With hundreds of books on the wall;
He drinks a great deal of Marsala,
    But never gets tipsy at all.

He has many friends, lay men and clerical,
  Old Foss is the name of his cat;
His body is perfectly spherical,
  He weareth a runcible hat.

When he walks in waterproof white,
  The children run after him so!
Calling out, 'He's gone out in his night-
  gown, that crazy old Englishman, oh!'

He weeps by the side of the ocean,
  He weeps on the top of the hill;
He purchases pancakes and lotion,
  And chocolate shrimps from the mill.

He reads, but he cannot speak, Spanish,
He cannot abide ginger beer:
Ere the days of his pilgrimage vanish,
  How pleasant to know Mr. Lear!

Edward Lear (1812–1888)

Song

Look not thou on beauty's charming,
Sit thou still when kings are arming,
Taste not when the wine-cup glistens,
Speak not when the people listens,
Stop thine ear against the singer,
From the red gold keep thy finger;
Vacant heart and hand and eye,
Easy live and quiet die.

Sir Walter Scott (1771–1832)

A Song of Joys

LINES 1–9

O to make the most jubilant song!
Full of music – full of manhood, womanhood, infancy!
Full of common employments – full of grain and trees.

O for the voices of animals – O for the swiftness and
balance of fishes!
O for the dropping of raindrops in a song!
O for the sunshine and motion of waves in a song!

O the joy of my spirit – it is uncaged – it darts like
lightning!
It is not enough to have this globe or a certain time,
I will have thousands of globes and all time.

Walt Whitman (1819–1892)

Inviting a Friend to Supper

To night, grave sir, both my poore house, and I
Doe equally desire your companie:
Not that we thinke us worthy such a ghest,
But that your worth will dignifie our feast,
With those that come; whose grace may make that seeme
Something, which else, could hope for no esteeme.
It is the faire acceptance, Sir, creates
The entertaynment perfect: not the cates.
Yet shall you have, to rectifie your palate,
An olive, capers, or some better sallade
Ushring the mutton; with a short-leg'd hen,
If we can get her, full of egs, and then
Limons, and wine for sauce: to these a coney
Is not to be despair'd of, for our money;
And, though fowle, now, be scarce, yet there are clarkes,
The skie not falling, thinke we may have larkes.
Ile tell you more, and lye, so you will come:
Of partrich, pheasant, wood-cock, of which some
May yet be there; and godwit, if we can:
Knat, raile, and ruffe too. How so ere, my man
Shall reade a piece of Virgil, Tacitus,
Livie, or of some better booke to us,
Of which wee'll speake our minds, amidst our meate;
And Ile professe no verses to repeate:
To this, if ought appeare which I not know of,

That will the pastrie, not my paper, show of.
Digestive cheese and fruit there sure will bee;
But that, which most doth take my Muse and mee,
Is a pure cup of rich Canary-wine,
Which is the Mermaids now, but shall be mine:
Of which had Horace, or Anacreon tasted,
Their lives, as doe their lines, till now had lasted.
Tobacco, Nectar, or the Thespian spring,
Are all but Luthers beere to this I sing.
Of this we will sup free, but moderately,
And we will have no Pooly', or Parrot by;
Nor shall our cups make any guiltie men;
But, at our parting we will be, as when
We innocently met. No simple word,
That shall be utter'd at our mirthfull boord,
Shall make us sad next morning: or affright
The libertie that wee'll enjoy to night.

Ben Jonson (1572–1637)

Home

Wherever on far distant farms
The orchard trees lift bounteous arms,
The lane is grape-leaved, woodland dense,
The chipmunk leaps the zigzag fence,
The horses from the plow's last round
Drink with a deep sweet cooling sound,
And with the thin young moon afloat
Comes up the frog's heart-easing note,
And tree-toads' endless melody,
 Oh, that is home,
 Is restful home to me.

Whenever on a distant street
Two charmful eyes I chance to meet,
The look of one that knows the grace
Of every change on nature's face,
Whose sea-like soul is open wide
To breezes from the farther side,
Whose voice and movement seem to give
The knowledge of how best to live
And how to live most happily,
 Oh, that is home,
 Is blessed home to me.

Ethelwyn Wetherald (1857–1940)

Aldworth House, Black Down

FROM *PROLOGUE TO GENERAL HAMLEY, THE CHARGE OF THE HEAVY BRIGADE AT BALACLAVA*

Our birches yellowing and from each
    The light leaf falling fast,
While squirrels from our fiery beech
    Were bearing off the mast,
You came, and look'd and loved the view
    Long-known and loved by me,
Green Sussex fading into blue
    With one gray glimpse of sea.

Alfred, Lord Tennyson (1809–1892)

The Kitten and Falling Leaves

LINES 1–40

That way look, my Infant, lo!
What a pretty baby-show!
See the Kitten on the wall,
Sporting with the leaves that fall,
Withered leaves – one – two – and three –
From the lofty elder-tree!
Through the calm and frosty air
Of this morning bright and fair,
Eddying round and round they sink
Softly, slowly: one might think,
From the motions that are made,
Every little leaf conveyed
Sylph or Faery hither tending, –
To this lower world descending,
Each invisible and mute,
In his wavering parachute.
– But the Kitten, how she starts,
Crouches, stretches, paws, and darts!
First at one, and then its fellow
Just as light and just as yellow;
There are many now – now one –
Now they stop and there are none.
What intenseness of desire

In her upward eye of fire!
With a tiger-leap half way
Now she meets the coming prey,
Lets it go as fast, and then
Has it in her power again:
Now she works with three or four,
Like an Indian conjurer;
Quick as he in feats of art,
Far beyond in joy of heart.
Were her antics played in the eye
Of a thousand standers-by,
Clapping hands with shout and stare,
What would little Tabby care
For the plaudits of the crowd?
Over happy to be proud,
Over wealthy in the treasure
Of her own exceeding pleasure!

William Wordsworth (1770–1850)

The Coming of Good Luck

So Good-luck came, and on my roofe did light,
Like noyse-lesse Snow; or as the dew of night;
Not all at once, but gently, as the trees
Are, by the Sun-beams, tickl'd by degrees.

Robert Herrick (1591–1674)

Drinking Song

There are people, I know, to be found,
   Who say, and apparently think,
That sorrow and care may be drowned
   By a timely consumption of drink.

Does not man, these enthusiasts ask,
   Most nearly approach the divine,
When engaged in the soul-stirring task
   Of filling his body with wine?

Have not beggars been frequently known,
   When satisfied, soaked, and replete,
To imagine their bench was a throne
   And the civilised world at their feet?

Lord Byron has finely described
   The remarkably soothing effect
Of liquor, profusely imbibed,
   On a soul that is shattered and wrecked.

In short, if your body or mind
   Or your soul or your purse come to grief,
You need only get drunk, and you'll find
   Complete and immediate relief.

For myself, I have managed to do
   Without having recourse to this plan,
So I can't write a poem for you,
   And you'd better get someone who can.

J. K. Stephen (1859–1892)

Song

When, dearest, I but think of thee,
Methinks all things that lovely be
   Are present, and my soul delighted:
For beauties that from worth arise
Are like the grace of deities,
   Still present with us, though unsighted.

Thus while I sit and sigh the day
With all his borrowed lights away,
   Till night's black wings do overtake me,
Thinking on thee, thy beauties then,
As sudden lights do sleepy men,
   So they by their bright rays awake me.

Thus absence dies, and dying proves
No absence can subsist with loves
   That do partake of fair perfection:
Since in the darkest night they may
By love's quick motion find a way
   To see each other by reflection.

The waving sea can with each flood
Bathe some high promont that hath stood
   Far from the main up in the river:
O think not then but love can do
As much! for that's an ocean too,
   Which flows not every day, but ever!

Sir John Suckling (1609–1642)

O Sweet Content

FROM *PATIENT GRISSIL*

Art thou poor, yet hast thou golden slumbers?
    O sweet content!
Art thou rich, yet is thy mind perplexed?
O punishment!
Dost thou laugh to see how fools are vexed
To add to golden numbers golden numbers?
O sweet content! O sweet content!
  Work apace, apace, apace, apace;
  Honest labour bears a lovely face;
 Then hey nonny nonny – hey nonny nonny!

Canst drink the waters of the crisped spring?
    O sweet content!
Swim'st thou in wealth, yet sink'st in thine own tears?
    O punishment!
Then he that patiently want's burden bears,
No burden bears, but is a king, a king!
O sweet content! O sweet content!
  Work apace, apace, apace, apace;
  Honest labour bears a lovely face;
 Then hey nonny nonny – hey nonny nonny!

Thomas Dekker (c. 1572–1632)

Sunday

Thou blessed day! I will not call thee last,
Nor Sabbath, – nor last nor first of all the seven,
But a calm slip of intervening heaven.
Between the uncertain future and the past;
As in a stormy night, amid the blast,
Comes ever and anon a truce on high,
And a calm lake of pure and starry sky
Peers through the mountainous depth of clouds amass'd.
Sweet day of prayer! e'en they whose scrupulous dread
Will call no other day, as others do,
Might call thee Sunday without fear or blame;
For thy bright morn deliver'd from the dead
Our Sun of Life, and will for aye renew
To faithful souls the import of thy name.

1843

Hartley Coleridge (1796–1849)

Happy the Man

FROM *THE ODES OF HORACE*, BOOK III

Happy the man, and happy he alone,
He who can call to-day his own:
  He who secure within, can say,
  Tomorrow do thy worst, for I have liv'd to-day.

  Be fair, or foul, or rain, or shine
  The Joys I have possess'd, in spite of Fate are mine.
Not Heaven it self upon the Past has Pow'r,
But what has been has been, and I have had my Hour.

John Dryden (1631–1700)

Heaven-Haven

A NUN TAKES THE VEIL

I have desired to go
   Where springs not fail,
To fields where flies no sharp and sided hail
   And a few lilies blow.

And I have asked to be
   Where no storms come,
Where the green swell is in the havens dumb,
   And out of the swing of the sea.

Gerard Manley Hopkins (1844–1889)

The Sunne Rising

Busie old foole, unruly Sunne,
   Why dost thou thus,
Through windowes, and through curtaines call on us?
Must to thy motions lovers seasons run?
   Sawcy pedantique wretch, goe chide
   Late school boyes, and sowre prentices,
  Goe tell Court-huntsmen, that the King will ride,
  Call countrey ants to harvest offices;
Love, all alike, no season knowes, nor clyme,
Nor houres, dayes, months, which are the rags of time.

   Thy beames, so reverend, and strong
   Why shouldst thou thinke?
I could eclipse and cloud them with a winke,
But that I would not lose her sight so long:
   If her eyes have not blinded thine,
   Looke, and to morrow late, tell mee,
  Whether both the'Indias of spice and Myne
  Be where thou leftst them, or lie here with mee.
Aske for those Kings whom thou saw'st yesterday,
And thou shalt heare, All here in one bed lay.

She is all States, and all Princes, I,
        Nothing else is.
Princes doe but play us; compar'd to this,
All honor's mimique; All wealth alchimie.
        Thou sunne art halfe as happy as wee,
        In that the world's contracted thus;
    Thine age askes ease, and since thy duties bee
    To warme the world, that's done in warming us.
Shine here to us, and thou art everywhere;
This bed thy center is, these walls, thy spheare.

John Donne (1572–1631)

When I Heard at the Close of the Day

When I heard at the close of the day how my name had
    been receiv'd with plaudits in the capitol, still it was
      not a happy night for me that follow'd,
And else when I carous'd, or when my plans were
    accomplish'd, still I was not happy,
But the day when I rose at dawn from the bed of perfect
    health, refresh'd, singing, inhaling the ripe breath of
    autumn,
When I saw the full moon in the west grow pale and
    disappear in the morning light,
When I wander'd alone over the beach, and undressing
    bathed, laughing with the cool waters, and saw
      the sun rise,
And when I thought how my dear friend my lover was
    on his way coming, O then I was happy,
O then each breath tasted sweeter, and all that day my
    food nourish'd me more, and the beautiful day
      pass'd well,

And the next came with equal joy, and with the next at
    evening came my friend,
And that night, while all was still I heard the waters roll
    slowly continually up the shores,
I heard the hissing rustle of the liquid and sands as
    directed to me whispering to congratulate me,
For the one I love most lay sleeping by me under the
    same cover in the cool night,
In the stillness in the autumn moonbeams his face was
    inclined toward me,
And his arm lay lightly around my breast – and that
    night I was happy.

Walt Whitman (1819–1892)

NOVEMBER

Twixt Air and Angels

The Treasure

When colour goes home into the eyes,
  And lights that shine are shut again
With dancing girls and sweet birds' cries
  Behind the gateways of the brain;
And that no-place which gave them birth, shall close
  The rainbow and the rose: –

Still may Time hold some golden space
  Where I'll unpack that scented store
Of song and flower and sky and face,
  And count, and touch, and turn them o'er,
Musing upon them; as a mother, who
Has watched her children all the rich day through
Sits, quiet-handed, in the fading light,
When children sleep, ere night.

August 1914

Rupert Brooke (1887–1915)

The Vagabond

TO AN AIR OF SCHUBERT

Give to me the life I love,
  Let the lave go by me,
Give the jolly heaven above
  And the byway night me.
Bed in the bush with stars to see,
  Bread I dip in the river –
There's the life for a man like me,
  There's the life for ever.

Let the blow fall soon or late,
  Let what will be o'er me;
Give the face of earth around
  And the road before me.
Wealth I seek not, hope nor love,
  Nor a friend to know me;
All I seek, the heaven above
  And the road below me.

Or let autumn fall on me
  Where afield I linger,
Silencing the bird on tree,
  Biting the blue finger;
White as meal the frosty field –
  Warm the fireside haven –
Not to autumn will I yield,
Not to winter even!

Let the blow fall soon or late,
  Let what will be o'er me;
Give the face of earth around,
  And the road before me.
Wealth I ask not, hope, nor love,
  Nor a friend to know me.
All I ask, the heaven above
  And the road below me.

Robert Louis Stevenson (1850–1894)

Charita

FROM *THE COUNTESS OF PEMBROKE'S ARCADIA*

My true love hath my hart, and I have his,
By just exchange, one for the other giv'ne.
I holde his deare, and myne he cannot misse:
There never was a better bargain driv'ne.

His hart in me, keepes me and him in one,
My hart in him, his thoughtes and senses guides:
He loves my hart, for once it was his owne:
I cherish his, because in me it bides.

His hart his wound receaved from my sight:
My hart was wounded, with his wounded hart,
For as from me, on him his hurt did light,
So still me thought in me his hurt did smart:
   Both equall hurt, in this change sought our blisse:
   My true love hath my hart and I have his.

Sir Philip Sidney (1554–1586)

Written in November

Autumn I love thy latter end to view
In cold novembers day so bleak and bare
When like lifes dwindld thread worn nearly thro
Wi lingering, pottering pace and head bleached bare
Thou like an old man bids the world adieu
I love thee well and often when a child
Have roamd the bare brown heath a flower to find
And in the moss clad vale and wood bank wild
Have cropt the little bell flowers paley blue
That trembling peept the sheltering bush behind
When winnowing north winds cold and blealy blew
How have I joyd wi dithering hands to find
Each fading flower and still how sweet the blast
Would bleak novembers hour Restore the joy thats past.

John Clare (1793–1864)

The Secret

In the profoundest ocean
There is a rainbow shell,
It is always there, shining most stilly
Under the greatest storm waves
That the old Greek called 'ripples of laughter.'
As you listen, the rainbow shell
Sings – in the profoundest ocean.
It is always there, singing most silently!

Katherine Mansfield (1888–1923)

A Boat Beneath a Sunny Sky

FROM *THROUGH THE LOOKING-GLASS*

A boat beneath a sunny sky,
Lingering onward dreamily
In an evening of July –

Children three that nestle near,
Eager eye and willing ear,
Pleased a simple tale to hear –

Long has paled that sunny sky:
Echoes fade and memories die:
Autumn frosts have slain July.

Still she haunts me, phantomwise,
Alice moving under skies
Never seen by waking eyes.

Children yet, the tale to hear,
Eager eye and willing ear,
Lovingly shall nestle near.

In a Wonderland they lie,
Dreaming as the days go by,
Dreaming as the summers die:

Ever drifting down the stream –
Lingering in the golden gleam –
Life, what is it but a dream?

Lewis Carroll (1832–1898)

Sonnet LXXV

FROM *AMORETTI*

One day I wrote her name upon the strand,
  but came the waves and washed it away:
  agayne I wrote it with a second hand,
  but came the tyde, and made my paynes his prey.
Vayne man, sayd she, that doest in vaine assay,
  a mortall thing so to immortalize
  for I my selve shall lyke to this decay,
  and eek my name bee wyped out lykewize.
Not so (quod I) let baser things devize
  to dy in dust, but you shall live by fame:
  my verse your vertues rare shall eternize,
  and in the hevens wryte your glorious name:
Where whereas death shall all the world subdew,
  our love shall live, and later life renew.

Edmund Spenser (c. 1552–1599)

The Hut by the Sea

Here is my hut beside the hilly sea,
  A sweet, small resting-place, so soft and warm,
Though framed by desolate immensity,
  And rocked within the arms of every storm.

Each home where love abides is even so,
  A steadfast joy beneath a changing sky;
And all the storms of life that round it blow
  Are but its cradle and its lullaby.

Ethelwyn Wetherald (1857–1940)

Aire and Angels

Twice or thrice had I loved thee,
Before I knew thy face or name;
So in a voice, so in a shapeless flame,
Angells affect us oft, and worship'd bee;
   Still when, to where thou wert, I came,
Some lovely glorious nothing I did see,
   But since, my soule, whose child love is,
Takes limmes of flesh, and else could nothing doe,
   More subtile than the parent is,
Love must not be, but take a body too,
   And therefore what thou wert, and who
     I did Love aske, and now
That it assume thy body, I allow,
And fix it selfe in thy lip, eye, and brow.

Whilst thus to ballast love, I thought,
And so more steddily to have gone,
With wares which would sinke admiration,
I saw, I had loves pinnace overfraught,
   Ev'ry thy haire for love to worke upon
Is much too much, some fitter must be sought;
   For, nor in nothing, nor in things
Extreme, and scattring bright, can love inhere;
   Then as an Angell, face, and wings
Of aire, not pure as it, yet pure doth weare,
   So thy love may be my loves spheare;
     Just such disparitie
As is twixt Air and Angells puritie,
'Twixt womens love, and mens will ever bee.

John Donne (1572–1631)

Celia, Celia

When I am sad and weary
When I think all hope has gone
When I walk along High Holborn
I think of you with nothing on.

Adrian Mitchell (1932–2008)

There Was a Boy

There was a boy – ye knew him well, ye cliffs
And islands of Winander – many a time
At evening, when the stars had just begun
To move along the edges of the hills,
Rising or setting, would he stand alone
Beneath the trees or by the glimmering lake,
And there, with fingers interwoven, both hands
Pressed closely palm to palm and to his mouth
Uplifted, he, as though an instrument,
Blew mimic hootings to the silent owls,
That they might answer him. And they would shout
Across the watery vale, and shout again,
Responsive to his call, with quavering peals,
And long halloos, and screams, and echoes loud,
Redoubled and redoubled – a wild scene
Of mirth and jocund din. And when it chanced
That pauses of deep silence mocked his skill,
Then sometimes in that silence, while he hung
Listening, a gentle shock of mild surprise
Has carried far into his heart the voice
Of mountain torrents; or the visible scene
Would enter unawares into his mind
With all its solemn imagery – its rocks,
Its woods, and that uncertain heaven – received
Into the bosom of the steady lake.

William Wordsworth (1770–1850)

Dining Room Tea

When you were there, and you, and you,
Happiness crowned the night; I too,
Laughing and looking, one of all,
I watched the quivering lamplight fall
On plate and flowers and pouring tea
And cup and cloth; and they and we
Flung all the dancing moments by
With jest and glitter. Lip and eye
Flashed on the glory, shone and cried,
Improvident, unmemoried;
And fitfully and like a flame
The light of laughter went and came.
Proud in their careless transience moved
The changing faces that I loved.

Till suddenly, and otherwhence,
I looked upon your innocence.
For lifted clear and still and strange
From the dark woven flow of change
Under a vast and starless sky
I saw the immortal moment lie.
One instant I, an instant, knew
As God knows all. And it and you
I, above Time, oh, blind! could see
In witless immortality.
I saw the marble cup; the tea,
Hung on the air, an amber stream;
I saw the fire's unglittering gleam,

The painted flame, the frozen smoke.
No more the flooding lamplight broke
On flying eyes and lips and hair;
But lay, but slept unbroken there,
On stiller flesh, and body breathless,
And lips and laughter stayed and deathless,
And words on which no silence grew.
Light was more alive than you.
For suddenly, and otherwhence,
I looked on your magnificence.
I saw the stillness and the light,
And you, august, immortal, white,
Holy and strange; and every glint
Posture and jest and thought and tint
Freed from the mask of transiency,
Triumphant in eternity,
Immote, immortal.

　　　　　Dazed at length
Human eyes grew, mortal strength
Wearied; and Time began to creep.
Change closed about me like a sleep.
Light glinted on the eyes I loved.
The cup was filled. The bodies moved.
The drifting petal came to ground.
The laughter chimed its perfect round.
The broken syllable was ended.
And I, so certain and so friended,
How could I cloud, or how distress,

The heaven of your unconsciousness?
Or shake at Time's sufficient spell,
Stammering of lights unutterable?
The eternal holiness of you,
The timeless end, you never knew,
The peace that lay, the light that shone.
You never knew that I had gone
A million miles away, and stayed
A million years. The laughter played
Unbroken round me; and the jest
Flashed on. And we that knew the best
Down wonderful hours grew happier yet.
I sang at heart, and talked, and eat,
And lived from laugh to laugh, I too,
When you were there, and you, and you.

Rupert Brooke (1887–1915)

November

Let baths and wine-butts be November's due,
   With thirty mule-loads of broad gold-pieces;
   And canopy with silk the streets that freeze;
And keep your drink-horns steadily in view.
Let every trader have his gain of you:
   Clareta shall your lamps and torches send,
   Caëta, citron-candies without end;
And each shall drink, and help his neighbour to.
And let the cold be great, and the fire grand:
   And still for fowls, and pastries sweetly wrought,
   For hares and kids, for roast and boiled, be sure
You always have your appetites at hand;
   And then let night howl and heaven fall, so nought
   Be missed that makes a man's bed-furniture.

Folgóre da San Gimignano (c. 1270–c. 1332)
Translated by Dante Gabriel Rossetti (1828–1882)

Song

There is dew for the flow'ret
  And honey for the bee,
And bowers for the wild bird,
  And love for you and me.

There are tears for the many
  And pleasures for the few;
But let the world pass on, dear,
  There's love for me and you.

Thomas Hood (1799–1845)

Song

Stay, stay at home, my heart, and rest;
Home-keeping hearts are happiest,
For those that wander they know not where
Are full of trouble and full of care;
   To stay at home is best.

Weary and homesick and distressed,
They wander east, they wander west,
And are baffled and beaten and blown about
By the winds of the wilderness of doubt;
   To stay at home is best.

Then stay at home, my heart, and rest;
The bird is safest in its nest;
O'er all that flutter their wings and fly
A hawk is hovering in the sky;
   To stay at home is best.

Henry Wadsworth Longfellow (1807–1882)

The Ruined Maid

'O 'Melia, my dear, this does everything crown!
Who could have supposed I should meet you in Town?
And whence such fair garments, such prosperi-ty?' –
'O didn't you know I'd been ruined?' said she.

– 'You left us in tatters, without shoes or socks,
Tired of digging potatoes, and spudding up docks;
And now you've gay bracelets and bright feathers three!' –
'Yes: that's how we dress when we're ruined,' said she.

– 'At home in the barton you said 'thee' and 'thou',
And 'thik oon', and theäs oon', and 't'other'; but now
Your talking quite fits 'ee for high compa-ny!' –
'Some polish is gained with one's ruin,' said she.

– 'Your hands were like paws then, your face blue and bleak
But now I'm bewitched by your delicate cheek,
And your little gloves fit as on any la-dy!' –
'We never do work when we're ruined,' said she.

– 'You used to call home-life a hag-ridden dream,
And you'd sigh, and you'd sock; but at present you seem
To know not of megrims or melancho-ly!' –
'True. One's pretty lively when ruined,' said she.

– 'I wish I had feathers, a fine sweeping gown,
And a delicate face, and could strut about Town!' –
'My dear – a raw country girl, such as you be,
Cannot quite expect that. You ain't ruined,' said she.

Westbourne Park Villas, 1866

Thomas Hardy (1840–1928)

Invitation to Love

Come when the nights are bright with stars
Or come when the moon is mellow;
Come when the sun his golden bars
Drops on the hay-field yellow.
Come in the twilight soft and gray,
Come in the night or come in the day,
Come, O love, whene'er you may,
And you are welcome, welcome.

You are sweet, O Love, dear Love,
You are soft as the nesting dove.
Come to my heart and bring it to rest
As the bird flies home to its welcome nest.

Come when my heart is full of grief
Or when my heart is merry;
Come with the falling of the leaf
Or with the redd'ning cherry.
Come when the year's first blossom blows,
Come when the summer gleams and glows,
Come with the winter's drifting snows,
And you are welcome, welcome.

Paul Laurence Dunbar (1872–1906)

Eternity

FROM *GNOMIC VERSES*

He who binds to himself a Joy
Doth the wingèd life destroy;
But he who kisses the Joy as it flies
Lives in Eternity's sunrise

William Blake (1757–1827)

November Skies

Than these November skies
Is no sky lovelier. The clouds are deep;
Into their grey the subtle spies
Of colour creep,
Changing that high austerity to delight,
Till even the leaden interfolds are bright.
And, where the cloud breaks, faint far azure peers
Ere a thin flushing cloud again
Shuts up that loveliness, or shares.
The huge great clouds move slowly, gently, as
Reluctant the quick sun should shine in vain,
Holding in bright caprice their rain.
And when of colours none,
Not rose, nor amber, nor the scarce late green,
Is truly seen, –
In all the myriad grey,
In silver height and dusky deep, remain
The loveliest,
Faint purple flushes of the unvanquished sun.

John Freeman (1880–1929)

If I Were

There are lots of ways to dance and
to spin, sometimes it just starts my
feet first then my entire body, I am
spinning no one can see it but it is
happening. I am so glad to be alive,
I am so glad to be loving and loved.
Even if I were close to the finish,
even if I were at my final breath, I
would be here to take a stand, bereft
of such astonishments, but for them.

If I were a Sufi for sure I would be
one of the spinning kind.

Mary Oliver (1935–2019)

Happy Thought

The world is full of a number of things,
I'm sure we should all be as happy as kings.

Robert Louis Stevenson (1850–1894)

Were I With You

Were I with you, or you with me,
My love, how happy should we be;
Day after day it is sad cheer
To have you there, while I am here.

My darling's face I cannot see,
My darling's voice is mute for me,
My fingers vainly seek the hair
Of her that is not here, but there.

In a strange land, to her unknown,
I sit and think of her alone;
And in that happy chamber where
We sat, she sits, nor has me there.

Yet still the happy thought recurs
That she is mine, as I am hers,
That she is there, as I am here,
And loves me, whether far or near.

The mere assurance that she lives
And loves me, full contentment gives;
I need not doubt, despond, or fear,
For, she is there, and I am here.

Arthur Hugh Clough (1819–1861)

Sussex

VERSES 1–3

1902

God gave all men all earth to love,
  But, since our hearts are small,
Ordained for each one spot should prove
  Belovèd over all;
That, as He watched Creation's birth,
  So we, in godlike mood,
May of our love create our earth
  And see that it is good.

So one shall Baltic pines content,
  As one some Surrey glade,
Or one the palm-grove's droned lament
  Before Levuka's Trade.
Each to his choice, and I rejoice
  The lot has fallen to me
In a fair ground – in a fair ground –
  Yea, Sussex by the sea!

No tender-hearted garden crowns,
  No bosomed woods adorn
Our blunt, bow-headed, whale-backed Downs,
  But gnarled and writhen thorn –
Bare slopes where chasing shadows skim,
  And, through the gaps revealed,
Belt upon belt, the wooded, dim,
  Blue goodness of the Weald.

Rudyard Kipling (1865–1936)

Happy the Man

FROM *A REVERIE*, LINES 45–58

'Ah! happy is the man whose early lot
Hath made him master of a furnished cot;
Who trains the vine that round his window grows,
And after setting sun his garden hoes;
Whose wattled pales his own enclosure shield,
Who toils not daily in another's field.
Where'er he goes, to church or market-town,
With more respect he and his dog are known;
A brisker face he wears at wake or fair,
Nor views with longing eyes the pedlar's ware,
But buys at will or ribbands, gloves or beads,
And willing maidens to the alehouse leads;
And, oh! secure from toils which cumber life,
He makes the maid he loves an easy wife.

Joanna Baillie (1762–1851)

The New England Boy's Song about Thanksgiving Day

Over the river and through the wood,
  To grandfather's house we go;
    The horse knows the way,
    To carry the sleigh,
  Through the white and drifted snow.

Over the river, and through the wood,
  To grandfather's house away!
    We would not stop
    For doll or top,
  For 'tis Thanksgiving Day.

Over the river, and through the wood,
  Oh, how the wind does blow!
    It stings the toes,
    And bites the nose,
  As over the ground we go.

Over the river, and through the wood,
  With a clear blue winter sky,
    The dogs do bark,
    And children hark,
  As we go jingling by.

Over the river, and through the wood,
　To have first-rate play –
　　Hear the bells ring,
　　Ting a ling ding,
　Hurra for Thanksgiving day!

Over the river, and through the wood –
　No matter for winds that blow;
　　Or if we get
　　The sleigh upset,
　Into a bank of snow.

Over the river, and through the wood,
　To see little John and Ann;
　　We will kiss them all
　　And play snow-ball,
　And stay as long as we can.

Over the river, and through the wood,
　Trot fast, my dapple grey!
　　Spring over the ground
　　Like a hunting hound,
　For 'tis Thanksgiving day!

Over the river, and through the wood,
  And straight through the barn-yard gate;
    We seem to go
    Extremely slow,
  It is so hard to wait.

Over the river, and through the wood –
  Old Jowler hears our bells;
    He shakes his pow
    With a loud bow wow,
  And thus the news he tells.

Over the river, and through the wood –
  When grandmother sees us come,
    She will say, 'O dear,
    The children are here,
  Bring a pie for everyone.'

Over the river and through the wood –
  Now grandmother's cap I spy!
    Hurra for the fun!
    Is the pudding done?
  Hurra for the pumpkin pie!

Lydia Maria Child (1802–1880)

Daybreak

All along the valley,
The mist of not-yet-morning
Folds the velvet cloak of dawn
Upon the distant hills,
Emerging from stillness
With a gentle yawn;
And frost-dampened shoulders
Shrug off the shrouds of night,
Wearing the first flush of violet
Beneath the day's first light.

Then grassy fields of blue,
Shivering softly
Beneath blankets of dew,
Slip slowly into
Emerald garments
As the blood-red
Sun arises.

How dreams, with reality
Are blurred
In this state of
Half-stirring, half-waking.
All is yet possible,
Redeemable,
As day is breaking.

Jana Synková (1968–)

'Henry comes! No sweeter music'

Henry comes! No sweeter music
  Ever strikes upon my ear
Than his dear advancing footstep,
  Which I sit and long to hear!

Henry comes! From toil returning,
  Sick of gloom and worldly strife,
O! let peace and joy attend him
  In the presence of a wife!

Hence then every bitter feeling!
  Hence each low and sordid care!
Let my thoughts be pure and gentle
  Fit for him I love to share!

Let my soul be fresh and bounding
  As the merry mountain brook,
Cheering him with tons of gladness,
  Yielding to his earnest look!

Like that clear transparent streamlet,
  All its liquid depths unclose,
And like that a faithful mirror
  Which his soul, reflecting, shows!

Sara Coleridge (1802–1852)

That Golden Time

When will it come, that golden time,
  When every man is free?
Men who have power to choose their tasks
  Have all their liberty.

They'll sweat and toil who love to feel
  Their muscles swell and move;
While men whose minds are more to them,
  Create the dreams we love.

When will it come, that golden time,
  When every heart must sing?
The power to choose the work we love
  Makes every man a king.

W. H. Davies (1871–1940)

Contentment

I like the way that the world is made,
   (Tickle me, please, behind the ears)
With part in the sun and part in the shade
   (Tickle me, *please*, behind the ears).
This comfortable spot beneath a tree
Was probably planned for you and me;
Why do you suppose God made a flea?
   Tickle me more behind the ears.

I hear a cricket or some such bug
   (Tickle me, please, behind the ears)
And there is a hole some creature dug
   (Tickle me, *please*, behind the ears).
I can't quite smell it from where we sit,
But I think a rabbit would hardly fit;
Tomorrow, perhaps, I'll look into it:
   Tickle me more behind the ears.

A troublesome fly is near my nose,
  (Tickle me, please, behind the ears);
He thinks I'll snap at him, I suppose,
  (Tickle me, *please*, behind the ears).
If I lay on my back with my legs in air
Would you scratch my stomach, just here and there?
It's a puppy trick and I don't much care,
  But tickle me more behind the ears.

Heaven, I guess, is all like this
  (Tickle me, please, behind the ears);
It's my idea of eternal bliss
  (Tickle me, *please*, behind the ears).
With angel cats for a dog to chase,
And a very extensive barking space,
And big bones buried all over the place, –
  And you, to tickle behind my ears.

Burges Johnson (1877–1963)

Wonder

VERSES 1–4

How like an angel came I down!
How bright are all things here!
When first among His works I did appear
Oh, how their glory me did crown!
The world resembled His eternity,
In which my soul did walk;
And everything that I did see
Did with me talk.

The skies in their magnificence,
The lively, lovely air;
Oh, how divine, how soft, how sweet, how fair!
The stars did entertain my sense,
And all the works of God, so bright and pure,
So rich and great did seem,
As if they ever must endure
In my esteem.

A native health and innocence
    Within my bones did grow,
And while my God did all His glories show,
    I felt a vigour in my sense
That was all spirit. I within did flow
    With seas of life, like wine;
    I nothing in the world did know
        But 'twas divine.

Harsh ragged objects were conceal'd,
    Oppressions tears and cries,
Sins, griefs, complaints, dissensions, weeping eyes
    Were hid, and only things revealed
Which heavenly spirits, and the angels prize.
    The state of innocence
    And bliss, not trades and poverties,
        Did fill my sense.

Thomas Traherne (1636/7–1674)

DECEMBER

Tidings of Comfort and Joy

Winter's Beauty

Is it not fine to walk in spring,
When leaves are born, and hear birds sing?
And when they lose their singing powers,
In summer, watch the bees at flowers?
Is it not fine, when summer's past,
To have the leaves, no longer fast,
Biting my heel where'er I go,
Or dancing lightly on my toe?
Now winter's here and rivers freeze;
As I walk out I see the trees,
Wherein the pretty squirrels sleep,
All standing in the snow so deep:
And every twig, however small,
Is blossomed white and beautiful.
Then welcome, winter, with thy power
To make this tree a big white flower;
To make this tree a lovely sight,
With fifty brown arms draped in white,
While thousands of small fingers show
In soft white gloves of purest snow.

W. H. Davies (1871–1940)

Endymion

BOOK I, LINES 1–24

A thing of beauty is a joy for ever:
Its loveliness increases; it will never
Pass into nothingness; but will still keep
A bower quiet for us, and a sleep
Full of sweet dreams, and health, and quiet breathing.
Therefore, on every morrow, we are wreathing
A flowery band to bind us to the earth,
Spite of despondence, of the inhuman dearth
Of noble natures, of the gloomy days,
Of all the unhealthy and o'er-darkened ways
Made for our searching: yes, in spite of all,
Some shape of beauty moves away the pall
From our dark spirits. Such the sun, the moon,
Trees old, and young, sprouting a shady boon
For simple sheep; and such are daffodils
With the green world they live in; and clear rills
That for themselves a cooling covert make
'Gainst the hot season; the mid forest brake,
Rich with a sprinkling of fair musk-rose blooms:
And such too is the grandeur of the dooms
We have imagined for the mighty dead;
All lovely tales that we have heard or read:
An endless fountain of immortal drink,
Pouring unto us from heaven's brink.

John Keats (1795–1821)

I'm Happiest When Most Away

I'm happiest when most away
I can bear my soul from its home of clay
On a windy night when the moon is bright
And the eye can wander through worlds of light

When I am not and none beside
Nor earth nor sea nor cloudless sky
But only spirit wandering wide
Through infinite immensity.

Emily Brontë (1818–1848)

To a Cat

PART I, VERSES 1–3

Stately, kindly, lordly friend,
  Condescend
Here to sit by me, and turn
Glorious eyes that smile and burn,
Golden eyes, love's lustrous meed,
On the golden page I read.

All your wondrous wealth of hair,
  Dark and fair,
Silken-shaggy, soft and bright
As the clouds and beams of night,
Pays my reverent hand's caress
Back with friendlier gentleness.

Dogs may fawn on all and some
  As they come;
You, a friend of loftier mind,
Answer friends alone in kind.
Just your foot upon my hand
Softly bids it understand.

Algernon Charles Swinburne (1837–1909)

Song

Through springtime walks, with flowers perfumed,
  I chased a wild capricious fair,
Where hyacinths and jonquils bloomed,
  Chanting gay sonnets through the air:
Hid amid a briary dell,
  Or 'neath a hawthorn tree,
Her sweet enchantments led me on,
  And still deluded me.

While summer's splendant glory smiles,
  My ardent love in vain essayed;
I strove to win her heart by wiles,
  But still a thousand pranks she played;
Still o'er each sun-burnt furzy hill,
  Wild, playful, gay and free,
She laughed and scorned, I chased her still,
  And still she bantered me.

When autumn waves her golden ears,
　　And wafts o'er fruits her pregnant breath,
The sprightly lark its pinions rears,
　　I chased her o'er the daisied heath;
Sweet harebells trembled in the vale,
　　And all around was glee;
Still, wanton as the timid hart,
　　She swiftly flew from me.

Now winter lights its cheerful fire,
　　While jests with frolic mirth resound,
And draws the wandering beauty nigher,
　　'Tis now too cold to rove around:
The Christmas game, the playful dance,
　　Incline her heart to glee;
Mutual we glow, and kindling love,
　　Draws every wish to me.

Anne Batten Cristall (1769–1848)

How a Little Girl Sang

Ah, she was music in herself,
A symphony of joyousness.
She sang, she sang from finger tips,
From every tremble of her dress.
I saw sweet haunting harmony,
An ecstasy, an ecstasy,
In that strange curling of her lips,
That happy curling of her lips.
And quivering with melody
Those eyes I saw, that tossing head.

And so I saw what music was,
Tho' still accursed with ears of lead.

Vachel Lindsay (1879–1931)

Epigram

The things that make a life to please
(Sweetest Martial), they are these:
Estate inherited, not got:
A thankful field, hearth always hot:
City seldom, law-suits never:
Equal friends agreeing ever:
Health of body, peace of mind:
Sleeps that till the morning bind:
Wise simplicity, plain fare:
Not drunken nights, yet loos'd from care:
A sober, not a sullen spouse:
Clean strength, not such as his that ploughs;
Wish only what you are, to be;
Death neither wish, nor fear to see.

Martial (c. 40–c. 103 AD)
Translated by Sir Richard Fanshawe (1608–1666)

The Means to Attain Happy Life

Martial, the things that do attain
The happy life, be these, I find:
The riches left, not got with pain,
The fruitful ground; the quiet mind:

The equal friend; no grudge, no strife;
No charge of rule, nor governance;
Without disease the healthful life;
The household of continuance:

The mean diet, no delicate fare;
True wisdom join'd with simpleness;
The night discharged of all care,
Where wine the wit may not oppress:

The faithful wife, without debate;
Such sleeps as may beguile the night:
Content thyself with thine estate,
No wish for death, no fear his might.

Henry Howard, Earl of Surrey (1517–1547)

Anniversary

What is sweeter than new-mown hay,
Fresher than winds o'er-sea that blow,
Innocent above children's play,
Fairer and purer than winter snow,
Frolic as are the morns of May?
　– If it should be what best I know!

What is richer than thoughts that stray
From reading of poems that smoothly flow?
What is solemn like the delay
Of concords linked in a music slow
Dying thro' vaulted aisles away?
　– If it should be what best I know!

What gives faith to me when I pray,
Setteth my heart with joy aglow,
Filleth my song with fancies gay,
Maketh the heaven to which I go,
The gladness of earth that lasteth for aye?
　– If it should be what best I know!

But tell me thou – 'twas on this day
That first we loved five years ago –
If 'tis a thing that I can say,
　Though it must be what best we know.

Robert Bridges (1844–1930)

437

Letters

FROM *EPISTLE TO HER FRIENDS AT GARTMORE*

If e'er my spirits want a flow,
Up stairs I run to my bureau,
And get your letters – read them over
With all the fondness of a lover;
This never fails to give me pleasure,
For these are Friendship's hoarded treasure,
And never fail to make me gay;
How oft I bless the happy day
Which made us friends and keeps us so,
Though now almost five years ago!
Trust me, my dear, I would not part
With the share, I hope, I've in your heart,
For any thing that wealth could give;
Without a friend, O who would live!
My favourite motto runs – 'He's poor
Who has a world and nothing more;
Exchange it for a friend, 'tis gain,
A better thing you then obtain.'

Susanna Blamire (1747–1794)

How Still, How Happy!

How still, how happy! Those are words
That once would scarce agree together;
I loved the plashing of the surge –
The changing heaven the breezy weather,

More than smooth seas and cloudless skies
And solemn, soothing, softened airs
That in the forest woke no sighs
And from the green spray shook no tears.

How still, how happy! Now I feel
Where silence dwells is sweeter far
Than laughing mirth's most joyous swell
However pure its raptures are.

Come, sit down on this sunny stone:
'Tis wintry light o'er flowerless moors –
But sit – for we are all alone
And clear expand heaven's breathless shores.

I could think in the withered grass
Spring's budding wreaths we might discern;
The violet's eye might shyly flash
And young leaves shoot among the fern.

It is but thought – full many a night
The snow shall clothe those hills afar
And storms shall add a drearier blight
And winds shall wage a wilder war,

Before the lark may herald in
Fresh foliage twined with blossoms fair
And summer days again begin
Their glory-haloed crown to wear.

Yet my heart loves December's smile
As much as July's golden beam;
Then let us sit and watch the while
The blue ice curdling on the stream.

Emily Brontë (1818–1848)

The Light Heart

(ITALIAN CHILD'S SONG)

I'd rather be a peasant
Without a care or sorrow
Than wear the Sultan's Crescent,
   Or be a Tartar Khan.
My oxen are the whitest
That till the Tuscan furrow,
My heart, my heart's the lightest
   From Naples to Milan!

I'd rather play with Lisa,
My little peasant-maiden,
Than own the Tower of Pisa
   Or dwell in Peter's Dome.
My lemon-trees are brightest,
My figs the heaviest-laden,
My heart, my heart's the lightest
   From Genoa to Rome!

Eleanor Farjeon (1881–1965)

Foure Things Make us Happy Here

Health is the first good lent to men;
A gentle disposition then:
Next, to be rich by no by-wayes;
Lastly, with friends t'enjoy our dayes.

Robert Herrick (1591–1674)

A Pebble

Drop a pebble in the water: just a splash, and it is gone;
But there's half-a-hundred ripples circling on and on
   and on,
Spreading, spreading from the center, flowing on out
   to the sea.
And there is no way of telling where the end is going
   to be.

Drop a pebble in the water: in a minute you forget,
But there's little waves a-flowing, and there's ripples
   circling yet,
And those little waves a-flowing to a great big wave
   have grown;
You've disturbed a mighty river just by dropping in
   a stone.

Drop an unkind word, or careless: in a minute it is gone;
But there's half-a-hundred ripples circling on and on
   and on.
They keep spreading, spreading, spreading from the
   center as they go,
And there is no way to stop them, once you've started
   them to flow.

Drop an unkind word, or careless: in a minute you
   forget;
But there's little waves a-flowing, and there's ripples
   circling yet,
And perhaps in some sad heart a mighty wave of tears
   you've stirred,
And disturbed a life was happy ere you dropped that
   unkind word.

Drop a word of cheer and kindness: just a flash and
   it is gone;
But there's half-a-hundred ripples circling on and on
   and on,
Bearing hope and joy and comfort on each splashing,
   dashing wave
Till you wouldn't believe the volume of the one kind
   word you gave.

Drop a word of cheer and kindness: in a minute you
   forget;
But there's gladness still a-swelling, and there's joy
   circling yet,
And you've rolled a wave of comfort whose sweet music
   can be heard
Over miles and miles of water just by dropping one
   kind word.

James W. Foley (1874–1939)

A Little Christmas Card

This little Christmas card has come,
  With greetings glad and gay,
To wish you all, both great and small,
  A merry Christmas Day.

Then when the festive day is past
  I'll just turn round, you see,
And wish you here a bright New Year,
  Quite full of mirth and glee.

And last your little Christmas card
  Will turn once more like this;
With smile so shy I'll say 'Good-bye,'
  And throw you each a kiss.

Anon

December

Last, for December, houses on the plain,
    Ground-floors to live in, logs heaped mountain-high,
    And carpets stretched, and newest games to try,
And torches lit, and gifts from man to man
(Your host, a drunkard and a Catalan;)
    And whole dead pigs, and cunning cooks to ply
    Each throat with tit-bits that shall satisfy;
And wine-butts of Saint Galganus' brave span.
And be your coats well-lined and tightly bound,
    And wrap yourselves in cloaks of strength and weight.
      With gallant hoods to put your faces through.
And make your game of abject vagabond
    Abandoned miserable reprobate
      Misers; don't let them have a chance with you.

Folgóre da San Gimignano (c. 1270–c. 1332)
Translated by Dante Gabriel Rossetti (1828–1882)

A Winter Song

VERSES 1–6, UNFINISHED

It is early morning within this room; without,
Dark and damp; without and within, stillness
Waiting for day: not a sound but a listening air.

Yellow jasmine, delicate on stiff branches
Stands in a Tuscan pot to delight the eye
In spare December's patient nakedness.

Suddenly, softly, as if at a breath breathed
On the pale wall, a magical apparition,
The shadow of the jasmine, branch and bloom!

It was not there, it is there, in a perfect image;
And all is changed. It is like a memory lost
Returning without a reason into the mind;

And it seems to me that the beauty of the shadow
Is more beautiful than the flower; a strange beauty,
Pencilled and silently deepening to distinctness.

As a memory stealing out of the mind's slumber,
A memory floating up from a dark water,
Can be more beautiful than the thing remembered.

Laurence Binyon (1869–1943)

The Orange

At lunchtime I bought a huge orange –
The size of it made us all laugh.
I peeled it and shared it with Robert and Dave –
They got quarters and I had a half.

And that orange, it made me so happy,
As ordinary things often do
Just lately. The shopping. A walk in the park.
This is peace and contentment. It's new.

The rest of the day was quite easy.
I did all the jobs on my list
And enjoyed them and had some time over.
I love you. I'm glad I exist.

Wendy Cope (1945–)

Character of a Happy Life

How happy is he born and taught
That serveth not another's will;
Whose armour is his honest thought,
And simple truth his utmost skill!

Whose passions not his masters are;
Whose soul is still prepared for death,
Untied unto the world by care
Of public fame or private breath;

Who envies none that chance doth raise,
Nor vice; who never understood
How deepest wounds are given by praise;
Nor rules of state, but rules of good;

Who hath his life from rumours freed;
Whose conscience is his strong retreat;
Whose state can neither flatterers feed,
Nor ruin make accusers great;

Who God doth late and early pray
More of His grace than gifts to lend;
And entertains the harmless day
With a well-chosen book or friend;

 – This man is freed from servile bands
Of hope to rise or fear to fall:
Lord of himself, though not of lands,
And having nothing, yet hath all.

Sir Henry Wotton (1568–1639)

In a Bath Teashop

'Let us not speak, for the love we bear one another –
  Let us hold hands and look.'
She, such a very ordinary little woman;
  He, such a thumping crook;
But both, for a moment, little lower than the angels
  In the teashop's ingle-nook.

John Betjeman (1906–1984)

Going Down Hill on a Bicycle

A Boy's Song

With lifted feet, hands still,
I am poised, and down the hill
Dart, with heedful mind;
The air goes by in a wind.

Swifter and yet more swift,
Till the heart with a mighty lift
Makes the lungs laugh, the throat cry –
'O bird, see; see, bird, I fly.

'Is this, is this your joy?
O bird, then I, though a boy,
For a golden moment share
Your feathery life in air!'

Say, heart, is there aught like this
In a world that is full of bliss?
'Tis more than skating, bound
Steel-shod to the level ground.

Speed slackens now, I float
Awhile in my airy boat;
Till, when the wheels scarce crawl,
My feet to the treadles fall.

Alas, that the longest hill
Must end in a vale; but still,
Who climbs with toil, wheresoe'er,
Shall find wings waiting there.

Henry Charles Beeching (1859–1919)

The Little Dancers

Lonely, save for a few faint stars, the sky
Dreams; and lonely, below, the little street
Into its gloom retires, secluded and shy.
Scarcely the dumb roar enters this soft retreat;
And all is dark, save where come flooding rays
From a tavern-window; there, to the brisk measure
Of an organ that down in the alley merrily plays,
Two children, all alone and no one by,
Holding their tattered frocks, thro' an airy maze
Of motion lightly threaded with nimble feet
Dance sedately; face to face they gaze,
Their eyes shining, grave with a perfect pleasure.

Laurence Binyon (1869–1943)

Ceremonies for Christmas

Come, bring with a noise,
　My merrie, merrie boyes,
The Christmas Log to the firing;
　While my good Dame, she
　Bids ye all be free;
And drink to your hearts desiring.

With the last yeeres brand
　Light the new block, And
For good success in his spending,
　On your Psaltries play,
　That sweet luck may
Come while the log is a teending.

Drink now the strong Beere,
　Cut the white loafe here,
The while the meat is a shredding;
　For the rare Mince-Pie
　And the Plums stand by
To fill the Paste that's a kneading.

Robert Herrick (1591–1674)

The Night Before Christmas

'Twas the night before Christmas, when all through the house
Not a creature was stirring, not even a mouse.
The stockings were hung by the chimney with care,
In hopes that St Nicholas soon would be there.
The children were nestled all snug in their beds,
While visions of sugar-plums danced in their heads.
And Mamma in her 'kerchief, and I in my cap,
Had just settled down for a long winter's nap,
When out on the lawn there arose such a clatter,
I sprang from my bed to see what was the matter.
Away to the window I flew like a flash,
Tore open the shutters and threw up the sash.
The moon on the breast of the new-fallen snow,
Gave a lustre of midday to objects below;
When, what to my wondering eyes should appear,
But a miniature sleigh and eight tiny reindeer,
With a little old driver, so lively and quick,
I knew in a moment he must be St Nick.
More rapid than eagles his coursers they came,
And he whistled, and shouted, and called them by name ...
'Now, Dasher! Now, Dancer!
Now, Prancer and Vixen!
On, Comet! On, Cupid!
On, Donner and Blitzen!
To the top of the porch!
To the top of the wall!
Now dash away! Dash away!
Dash away all!'
As dry leaves that before the wild hurricane fly,
When they meet with an obstacle, mount to the sky;
So up to the house-top the coursers they flew

With the sleigh full of toys – and St Nicholas, too.
And then, in a twinkling, I heard on the roof
The prancing and pawing of each little hoof.
As I drew in my head and was turning around,
Down the chimney St Nicholas came with a bound.
He was dressed all in fur, from his head to his foot,
And his clothes were all tarnished with ashes and soot.
A bundle of toys he had flung on his back,
And he looked like a pedlar just opening his pack.
His eyes – how they twinkled! his dimples, how merry!
His cheeks were like roses, his nose like a cherry!
His droll little mouth was drawn up like a bow,
And the beard on his chin was as white as the snow!
The stump of a pipe he held tight in his teeth,
And the smoke it encircled his head like a wreath.
He had a broad face and a little round belly
That shook when he laughed, like a bowl full of jelly.
He was chubby and plump – a right jolly old elf,
And I laughed when I saw him, in spite of myself.
A wink of his eye and a twist of his head
Soon gave me to know I had nothing to dread.
He spoke not a word, but went straight to his work,
And filled all the stockings, then turned with a jerk ...
And laying his finger aside of his nose,
And giving a nod, up the chimney he rose.
He sprang to his sleigh, to his team gave a whistle,
And away they all flew like the down of a thistle.
But I heard him exclaim, as he drove out of sight,
'Merry Christmas to all, and to all a good night!'

Clement Clarke Moore (1779–1863)

God Rest Ye, Merry Gentleman

VERSE 1

God rest ye, merry Gentlemen,
Let nothing you dismay,
For Jesus Christ our Saviour
Was born upon this Day.
To save poor souls from Satan's power
Which long time had gone astray.
Oh, tidings of comfort and joy
Comfort and joy.
Oh tidings of comfort and joy.

Anon

First Fig

My candle burns at both ends;
   It will not last the night;
But ah, my foes, and oh, my friends –
   It gives a lovely light!

Edna St Vincent Millay (1892–1950)

To Joy

Lo, I am happy, for my eyes have seen
Joy glowing here before me, face to face;
His wings were arched above me for a space,
I kissed his lips, no bitter came between.
The air is vibrant where his feet have been,
And full of song and color is his place.
His wondrous presence sheds about a grace
That lifts and hallows all that once was mean.
I may not sorrow for I saw the light,
Tho' I shall walk in valley ways for long,
I still shall hear the echo of the song, –
My life is measured by its one great height.
Joy holds more grace than pain can ever give,
And by my glimpse of joy my soul shall live.

Sara Teasdale (1884–1933)

O What Unhop't for Sweet Supply

O what unhop't for sweet supply!
  O what joyes exceeding!
What an affecting charme feele I,
  From delight proceeding!
That which I long despair'd to be,
To her I am, and shee to mee.

Shee that alone in cloudy griefe
  Long to mee appeared:
Shee now alone with bright reliefe
  All those clouds hath cleared.
Both are immortall, and divine,
  Since I am hers, and she is mine.

Thomas Campion (1567–1620)

Merry-Go-Round

Purple horses with orange manes
  Elephants pink and blue,
Tigers and lions that never were seen
  In circus parade or zoo!
Bring out your money and choose your steed,
  And prance to delightsome sound.
What fun if the world would turn some day
  Into a Merry-Go-Round!

Rachel Field (1894–1942)

Rondeau

Jenny kissed me when we met,
   Jumping from the chair she sat in;
Time, you thief, who love to get
   Sweets into your list, put that in:
Say I'm weary, say I'm sad,
   Say that health and wealth have missed me,
Say I'm growing old, but add,
   Jenny kissed me.

Leigh Hunt (1784–1859)

Three Things to Remember

As long as you're dancing, you can
   break the rules.
Sometimes breaking the rules is just
   extending the rules.

Sometimes there are no rules.

Mary Oliver (1935–2019)

Index of First Lines

I'll tell you how the Sun rose – 188
I'm glad the sky is painted blue 304
I'm happiest when most away 430
In February I give you gallant sport 58
In June I give you a close-wooded fell 212
In March I give you plenteous fisheries 106
In the middle of our porridge plates 60
In the profoundest ocean 393
In the time of old sin without sadness 211
Into my heart an air that kills 313
Into the scented woods we'll go 91
Is it not fine to walk in spring 428
It is a flaw 224
It is early morning within this room; without 447
It was a lover and his lass 129
It was a perfect day 90

Jacke and Jone they thinke no ill 325–6
Jenny kissed me when we met 462
Journeying on high, the silken castle glides 16
Joy, how I sought thee! 169
Just a few of the roses we gathered from the Isar 216

Last, for December, houses on the plain 446
Let baths and wine-butts be November's due 403
Let Beauty awake in the morn from beautiful dreams 318
Let us, as by this verdant bank we float 230
'Let us not speak, for the love we bear one another – 450
Let us walk in the white snow 14
Life, believe, is not a dream 275
Little tube of mighty pow'r 119
Lo, I am happy, for my eyes have seen 459
Lo, when we wade the tangled wood 264
Lonely, save for a few faint stars, the sky 453
Look at the stars! look, look up at the skies! 171
Look not thou on beauty's charming 367
Lord, when I look at lovely things which pass 111
Love said, 'Lie still and think of me,' 48
Loveliest of trees, the cherry now 149
Lovely kind, and kindly loving 131
Low-anchored cloud 178
Lying flat in the bracken of Richmond Park 213

Make new friends, but keep the old 184
Martial, the things that do attain 436
Me clairvoyant 210
'Mid pleasures and palaces though we may roam 323
Miss J. Hunter Dunn, Miss J. Hunter Dunn 301–2

The fairy beam upon you 107
The feildes are grene, the springe growes on a-pace 190
The first surprise: I like it 35
The grey sea and the long black land 331
The happy white throat on the sweeing bough 128
The idle life I lead 102
The neighbour sits in his window and plays the flute 57
The optimist builds himself safe inside a cell 34
The Owl and the Pussycat went to sea 32–3
The Persian's flowery gifts, the shrine 344
The railroad track is miles away 41
The recipe for a good margarita 240–1
The sea was sapphire coloured, and the sky 132
The summer down the garden walks 219
The sun upon the lake is low 343
The sweetest thing, I thought 136
The things that make a life to please 435
The unanimous Declaration of the thirteen united States 237
The wind blows happily on every thing 183
The wind may blow the snow about 29
The world is full of a number of things 412
The year's at the spring 88
Then hath thy orchard fruit, thy garden flowers 315
There are lots of ways to dance and 411
There are people, I know, to be found 376
There is a band of dull gold in the west, and say 351
There is a path that leads from every one's door into the 160
There is dew for the flow'ret 404
There is no architect 148
There is no happier life 103
There is pleasure in the wet, wet clay 110
There is sweet music here that softer falls 238
'There isn't much cricket in the Cromwell play.' 161–2
There was a boy – ye knew him well, ye cliffs 399
There was such beauty in the dappled valley 146
These dolphins twisting each on either side 311
They went away, the sad times 258
This is the hill, ringed by the misty shire – 310
This is the spot: – how mildly does the sun 339
This little Christmas card has come 445
This morning when the dew was chill 174–5
This way, this way, come and hear 13
Thou blessed day! I will not call thee last 379
Through springtime walks, with flowers perfumed 432–3
Through the ample open door of the peaceful country barn 228
'Tis mirth that fils the veins with bloud 80
'Tis the human touch in this world that counts 321
To make this condiment your poet begs 191

470

To night, grave sir, both my poore house, and I 369–70
To sea, to sea! The calm is o'er 337
'Twas the night before Christmas, when all through the house
     455–6
Twice or thrice had I loved thee 397

Under a flowering Tree 239
Up! up! my Friend, and quit your books 118
Upon the water, in the boat 199

We have a little garden 297
We have no grass locked up in ice so fast 30
We were very tired, we were very merry – 244
Well then! I now do plainly see 113–14
Were I with you, or you with me 413
What harvest halfe so sweet is 299
What is sweeter than new-mown hay 437
What wond'rous Life is this I lead! 319–20
What's the best thing in the world 193
When a felon's not engaged in his employment 66
When colour goes home into the eyes 388
When, dearest, I but think of thee 377
When I am sad and weary 398
When I but hear her sing, I fare 49
When I heard at the close of the day how my name had 384–5
When June is come, then all the day 198
When love with unconfinèd wings 134–5
When MAY is in his prime, then may each heart rejoice 177
When Mrs Gorm (Aunt Eloise) 179
When music sounds, gone is the earth I know 112
When someone's happy in a house there shows 101
When the sweet Poison of the Treacherous Grape 115
When will it come, that golden time 421
When wintry weather's all a-done 142
When you were there, and you, and you 400–2
Where innocent bright-eyed daisies are 217
Where the bee sucks, there suck I 267
Where the pools are bright and deep 165
Wherever on far distant farms 371
Who can live in heart so glad 89
Who goes amid the green wood 130
Who smoke-snorts toasts o' My Lady Nicotine 209
Why should my anxious breast repine 44
Why, who makes much of a miracle 250–1
Winter is a social season 17
With freedom, books, flowers, and the moon, who could 170
With lifted feet, hands still 451–2
With rakish eye and plenished crop 124

Index of Poets

Sources

Fleur Adcock, 'Londoner', from *Poems, 1960–2000*, Bloodaxe Books, 2000. Reproduced by permission of Bloodaxe Books.

Simon Armitage, 'The Catch', from *Kid*, Faber, 1992. Reprinted by permission of Faber and Faber Ltd.

Edmund Clerihew Bentley, 'Contentment'. Reproduced with permission of Curtis Brown Group Ltd, London, on behalf of the Estate of E.C. Bentley. Copyright © E. C. Bentley 1983

John Betjeman, 'In a Bath Teashop', 'A Subaltern's Love-Song' and 'Seaside Golf' from *Collected Poems*, John Murray, 1979. Reproduced with permission of the Licensor through PLSClear.

Edmund Blunden, 'The Surprise', from *Selected Poems*, Carcanet, 1982. Reprinted by kind permission of Carcanet Press, Manchester, UK.

Wendy Cope, 'After Lunch' and 'On a Train' from *Two Cures for Love: Selected Poems 1979–2006*, Faber, 2009. 'The Orange' and 'The Cricketing Versions' from *Serious Concerns*, Faber, 2019. Reprinted by permission of Faber and Faber Ltd and United Artists.

Frances Cornford, 'Summer Beach' from *Collected Poems*, Cresset Press, 1954; 'After the Examination' from *Selected Poems*, Enitharmon Press, 1996. Reprinted with the permission of the trustees of the Frances Crofts Cornford Will Trust.

Walter de la Mare, 'Music' from *Motley and Other Poems*, Constable, 1918; 'No Bed' and 'Puss' from *Collected Rhymes and Verses*, Faber, 1956. Reprinted with the permission of The Literary Trustees of Walter de la Mare and the Society of Authors as their Representative.

Gavin Ewart, 'June 1966' from *Selected Poems 1933–1993*, Hutchinson, 1996. Reprinted by permission of Jane Ewart.

U. A. Fanthorpe, 'Men on Allotments' from *Selected Poems*, Peterloo Press, 1986. Reprinted by kind permission of Dr R. V. Bailey.

Eleanor Farjeon, 'The Light Heart', 'The Girl with the Ball', 'A Morning Song' and 'Cats' from *The Children's Bells*, Oxford University Press, 1972. Reproduced by permission of David Higham Associates.

Elain Feinstein, 'Getting Older' and 'Photographs' from *Selected Poems*, Carcanet Press, 1994. Reprinted by kind permission of Carcanet Press, Manchester, UK.

Kathleen Jamie, 'The Wishing Tree' from *The Tree House*, Picador, 2004. Reproduced with permission of the Licensor through PLSClear.

Laurie Lee, 'April Rise' from *Selected Poems*, Unicorn Press, 2014. Reproduced with permission of Curtis Brown Ltd, London, on behalf of the Estate of Laurie Lee. Copyright © The Estate of Laurie Lee 1940.

Norman MacCaig, 'Emblems: after her illness' and 'Edinburgh Stroll' from *The Many Days*, Polygon, 2010. Reproduced with permission of the Licensor through PLSClear.

Acknowledgements

As always, a huge thank you to everyone at Hatchards for looking after my books so well. Louy and David Piachaud, Sue and David Gibb, Ian Prince and Julie Apps yet again came up with helpful suggestions, poems I didn't know and others I had forgotten. My editors at Batsford, Tina Persaud and Nicola Newman, make compiling these anthologies a true pleasure. Matilda, my small grey tabby cat, has been more hindrance than help but has brought much happiness while I work.

ABOUT THE AUTHOR

Jane McMorland Hunter has compiled ten anthologies for Batsford and the National Trust, including collections on gardening, nature, friendship, London, England and the First World War. She has also worked as a gardener, potter and quilter, writes gardening, cookery and craft books and works at Hatchards Bookshop in Piccadilly. She was brought up in the country, but now lives happily in London, in a house overflowing with books and a small garden overflowing with plants.